DEVOTIONS®

JUNE

 For the LORD loves the just and will not forsake his faithful ones. They will be protected forever.

—*Psalm 37:28*

Gary Allen, Editor   **Margaret Williams,** Project Editor   Photo © Dennizin | Dreamstime.com

DEVOTIONS® is published quarterly by Standard Publishing, Cincinnati, Ohio, www.standardpub.com. © 2011 by Standard Publishing. All rights reserved. Topics based on the Home Daily Bible Readings, International Sunday School Lessons. © 2008 by the Committee on the Uniform Series. Printed in the U.S.A. All Scripture quotations, unless otherwise indicated, are taken from the *HOLY BIBLE, NEW INTERNATIONAL VERSION*®. *NIV*®. Copyright © 1973, 1978, 1984 by Biblica Inc.™ Used by permission of Zondervan. All rights reserved. Where noted, Scripture quotations are from the following, used with permission of the copyright holders, all rights reserved: *King James Version (KJV),* public domain. *Holy Bible, New Living Translation (NLT),* © 1996. Tyndale House Publishers. *New American Standard Bible (NASB),* © The Lockman Foundation, 1960, 1962, 1963, 1968, 1971, 1972, 1973, 1975, 1977, 1995.

His Way

Whether you turn to the right or to the left, your ears will hear a voice behind you, saying, "This is the way; walk in it" (Isaiah 30:21).

Scripture: Isaiah 30:18-22
Song: "I Heard the Voice of Jesus Say"

"Turn! Turn right," my husband's friends hollered at him. Chet swung off the highway onto the side road. "Were you sleeping?" the guys asked. "You almost missed our turnoff."

"Sorry. I didn't see the sign," Chet said.

"You'd better get your eyes checked," Tom said.

Something similar seemed to happen to God's people in Judah. They too were on the wrong road, but they needed more than an eye checkup. Isaiah called them an obstinate people. "Turn to the Lord," he said. "Repent. Trust God. He will be gracious to you and will answer you."

Sometimes we do our own thing on a road to nowhere. It takes a friend, a sermon, or a tragedy to open our ears to God's voice. Turn. Turn right. "This is the way; walk in it" (v. 21).

If we listen we'll hear Jesus say, "I am the way and the truth and the life" (John 14:6). The New Testament calls us to repent. Next, we must accept Jesus as Lord. Finally, let us walk as He did in love.

Loving Father, thank You for Jesus who is the way to You. He gave himself for our sins, and by repentance we have a clear path to Heaven. But let us be attentive to the voice telling us, "This is the way; walk in it." In Jesus' name, amen.

June 1–3. **Elizabeth Van Liere** lives in Montrose, Colorado, and feels blessed by God to live close to the beautiful San Juan Mountains.

Rocky Beauty

He is the Rock, his works are perfect, and all his ways are just (Deuteronomy 32:4).

Scripture: Deuteronomy 31:30–32:7
Song: "The Solid Rock"

My husband and I were rock hounds. Chet said the most interesting ones were the ugly, round, baseball-sized ones. *How odd*, I thought. But, as a good partner, I bagged several and helped lug those heavy rocks home. The next day Chet began to cut one in half with an electric saw.

Hours later, he called me. "This is a geode," he explained.

"Wow!" I gasped. There, in that ugly rock, lay a lovely, miniature crystal garden.

Chet cut two more. Duds—just plain old rocks. Two others were glassy-smooth, rocky shells with agate fillings. "Thunder eggs," Chet said.

Rock hunting is a great hobby. Hopefully, inside those round, ugly ones you will find lovely surprises 90% of the time.

Moses points us to God, the Rock who is always breathtaking. Unlike the rocks we dug from cliffs, there will never be any question of a surprise with Him.

His ways are perfect. He is just. He is faithful and upright.

Moses sang such praises to the Rock, who is God himself. Can we do less?

My Rock and my God, I find it difficult to sing praises worthy of You. Words fail me. I can only bow down and say thank You for being such a Rock, one who never changes. Above all, You are the one who loves us so much that You sent Your Son to open our hearts to that love. Thank You, Father, in the name of Jesus. Amen.

Forgiveness for the Heartbroken

I will not acquit the guilty (Exodus 23:7).

Scripture: Exodus 23:1-9
Song: "Search Me, Know Me"

How scary! God says He will not absolve the guilt of those who disobey the laws of justice and mercy. Surely, I am not guilty.

But wait! How about joining the crowd in wrongdoing? Ouch . . . It happened when I was a senior in high school. A popular group decided to go against the rules and skip school the next day. Someone asked, "I suppose you won't go?"

At once the words fell from my lips. "Yes, I'll go."

"That's a surprise," the girl said. Her words burned in my heart. I had taken Jesus as my Savior and tried to show it by the way I lived. Now the "I'll go" rang loudly in my ears. Was it because I had been asked by somebody in the "in crowd"?

After a sleepless night I decided: No, I won't go. I told God I was sorry about my earlier yes. With a slightly upset stomach, I left for school, expecting plenty of sarcastic remarks.

I got off easy. Our "skip day" had been called off.

I am no longer scared of being judged guilty. God doesn't remember it as I do; I sincerely asked for forgiveness. He won't acquit the unrepentant guilty, but in His great mercy He forgives the heartbroken sinner.

Forgiving Father, I've had to ask for forgiveness many times since that day long ago. I am sorry I keep sinning over and over. Help me, God, for I am weak. I thank You for forgiveness, possible only because of the sacrifice of Jesus, my Lord. In His name I pray. Amen.

Stand in the Gap

I looked for a man among them who would build up the wall and stand before me in the gap on behalf of the land so I would not have to destroy it (Ezekiel 22:30).

Scripture: Ezekiel 22:23-31
Song: "Standing in the Gap"

"A stone wall surrounded the pasture, but there was no gate," Robert explained to me. He was telling about his walking tour of Ireland. "There was a gap in the wall where the gate should have been," Robert continued. "Near the gap was a modern-day shepherd. I asked the shepherd, 'What happened to the gate?'"

"He looked me in the eye," said Robert, "and told me: I am the gate." It was the shepherd's job to keep the sheep safe. In this case, he guarded the entrance to the pasture himself, by standing in the gap.

There was a gap in the wall in Ezekiel's day too. And God looked for someone to build up the wall and stand in the gap. Who would defend the poor, provide for the widow, or be kind to the foreigner? There was no justice in the land.

Jesus stands in the gap for us. He is our shepherd, our protector, our defender, and our redeemer. His love is so consuming and overwhelming that He died to save us. He cares for the oppressed, and He wants us to care for them too.

Shepherd of my Heart, You stand in the gap for me. Give me Your eyes of compassion to see people as You see them. In Your precious name, amen.

June 4–10. **Julie Kloster** is a teacher and freelance writer who lives with her husband and three daughters in Sycamore, Illinois. Her most recent Bible study is *The Eternal Truths of Narnia.*

Faith Actions

While you were doing all these things, declares the LORD, I spoke to you again and again, but you did not listen; I called you, but you did not answer (Jeremiah 7:13).

Scripture: Jeremiah 7:8-15
Song: "Follow You"

"True faith requires action," Dad said as he poured bottles of alcohol down the kitchen sink and crushed his cigarette pack. At 37 years of age, my dad heard God's call, and he responded. His unhealthy habits were replaced with a passion to follow Jesus. Dad studied the Scriptures, and his personal relationship with his Savior deepened as he sought heavenly guidance.

Thirty-five years later, Dad's love and passion for Christ continues to drive his ministry. God leads him to provide assistance to the poor, encourage the addicted, teach Bible classes, and minister to prisoners. Many people have become followers of Christ through my dad's ministries, because his life reflects the love and compassion of Jesus. Dad's faith is not a "Sunday only" religion. Jesus permeates his life.

In today's passage the Israelites believed they were safe because they worshipped in the temple, but their lives didn't reflect a passion for God. In mercy God called to them again and again, but they failed to hear. So I ask myself today: Do I listen to God so that I have a vibrant, personal walk with Him daily?

Merciful Father, thank You for calling me to a right relationship with You through Christ. Today I renew my commitment to be Your follower. Please give me the strength I need to live a vibrant, Christ-filled life every day. Let my actions prove my faith. I will follow You, for I am Yours. In Jesus' name, amen.

Mercy's Cry

O LORD, I say to you, "You are my God." Hear, O Lord, my cry for mercy (Psalm 140:6).

Scripture: Psalm 140:1-8
Song: "Rescue the Perishing"

"I realized that for the price of a good silk blouse I could save a kid's life," said Olga Murray. In 1984 Murray had taken a vacation and had walked through the impoverished villages of Nepal that were located in the shadows of the Himalayan Mountains. As a result of that trip, Murray began the Nepalese Youth Opportunity Foundation.

The foundation has rescued over 9,000 girls from slavery and has educated thousands of others. Nepalese girls as young as 6 years old are sold to work as indentured servants, who are often mistreated and abused. For over 25 years, Olga's organization has provided rescue, education, health care, and housing to Nepal.

God has many ways to rescue His people from the evils of this world. The psalmist in today's passage understood that God was his ultimate rescuer. Though the methods of rescue vary, usually making use of human hands, God is the one who inspires the mercy.

Is there injustice in my life? I must seek God's mercy to endure the hardship. Do I see injustice in the lives of others? May I search God's heart for wisdom to know how to help.

God, hear my cry for mercy, for You are my strong deliverer. Give me the grace to endure hardships caused by injustice. Protect me from the hands of evil, and give me compassion to help others. My hope and my trust are in You. In Jesus' name, amen.

Precious in His Sight

Whoever welcomes a little child like this in my name welcomes me (Matthew 18:5).

Scripture: Matthew 18:1-9
Song: "Jesus Loves the Little Children"

"Do you know my mom is in the hospital?" I shaded my eyes from the glare of the public pool and saw Desi standing near my poolside chair. My family had attended church with Desi and her mom three years earlier, but we had lost contact with each other. Desi was 10, the same age as my youngest daughter.

"No, I didn't know. Do you live here in Sycamore now?" I asked Desi.

She nodded. "Mom and I live over there." She pointed in the direction of a run-down trailer park that often flooded.

Desi's mom had stage four cancer and only lived one more year after this conversation. During that year, God called His people to minister to Desi and her mother. The night her mom died, Desi was in my arms.

After the funeral, Desi was welcomed into the home of relatives who lived in another town. Our church developed a ministry to people in the trailer park where Desi and her mom had lived. This ministry includes food delivery, children's programs, and temporary shelter.

Children are precious to Jesus. When we receive a child in His name, it is just as if we receive Christ himself.

Lord, I come to Your open arms with the faith and trust of a child. I am eager to learn from You. Please show me Your ways. Let my life be such a reflection of You that children are drawn into Your arms when I minister in Your name. Through Christ, amen.

His Unfailing Promises

This is what the LORD Almighty, the God of Israel, says: Reform your ways and your actions, and I will let you live in this place (Jeremiah 7:3).

Scripture: Jeremiah 7:1-7
Song: "Blood of His Covenant"

"Put your John Hancock on the dotted line," I quipped. My fifth-grade student signed his name with a flourish and a grin. "Do you understand your part of the behavior contract?" I asked. He nodded emphatically.

In public schools, behavior contracts are a great tool to help students take responsibility for themselves. The contract spells out expected classroom behaviors and then explains the rewards of good conduct. If the students fulfill their contracts, they "cash in" on the promised reward.

The prophet Jeremiah explained God's behavioral expectations for living in the promised land. The Israelites didn't keep their covenant with God, however, so they eventually suffered deportation from their homes.

God is merciful, and He made a new covenant. This time the covenant was for all people. Jesus died on the cross for our sins so we can have eternal life. Do we have a part in this new covenant? Yes! We must simply accept His free gift of eternal life and follow Christ with all of our hearts. The covenant fulfillment rests on God, and He always keeps His promises.

Covenant- keeping God, I am so grateful that You always keep Your promises. Even when I fall short, You provide a way for me to have fellowship with You through Christ. It is in His name I pray. Amen.

Mercy-bent Faith

"Which of these three do you think was a neighbor to the man who fell into the hands of robbers?" The expert in the law replied, "The one who had mercy on him." Jesus told him, "Go and do likewise" (Luke 10:36, 37).

Scripture: Luke 10:25-37
Song: "Give Me Your Eyes"

"We hit the deck when we hear gunshots," my sister-in-law, Beth, told me. She and her family live in the inner city of Chicago. They are urban missionaries carrying out the commands of Jesus to love their neighbor.

When the apartment building next door to them burned down, the lot was sold to Beth and her husband, Russ, for $1.00. They turned it into a private, supervised neighborhood park where children could come to play in safety from guns and violence. Beth also opens her home to neighborhood children after school for "Homework Club." Latchkey children come to her house for homemade cookies and a quiet place to study with tutoring help. Students can also sign up for classes in cooking, sewing, and computer. So many children want to sign up that classes are offered on a first-come, first-serve basis.

"All of us are missionaries," Beth explained to me. "We must take seriously God's command to love our neighbor. We are the hands and feet of Jesus to the hurting world."

Merciful Father, thank You for Your compassion. Give me Your eyes to see opportunities to serve You through ministry to those who are hurting. Forgive me for the times I have ignored someone's pain because I am unconcerned or too busy. Mold my heart to be mercy-bent. In the name of Your Son, my Savior, I pray. Amen.

International Doorstep

The alien living with you must be treated as one of your native-born. Love him as yourself, for you were aliens in Egypt. I am the LORD your God (Leviticus 19:34).

Scripture: Leviticus 19:9-18, 33-37
Song: "We've a Story to Tell to the Nations"

"I have lived in the USA for five years, but this is the first time I've been invited into the home of an American citizen," Chang said as I welcomed him at the door of my home.

Chang's girlfriend, Lan, nodded. "He's so happy today. He's been jealous because I had you as American friends as soon as I arrived from China." Chang laughed and nodded in agreement.

Our family had "adopted" Lan as part of a host program at Northern Illinois University. During the first month of Lan's arrival, we had met over frozen custard in waffle cones at our locally famous treat shop, Ollies. Eventually, Lan asked us if we wanted to meet her boyfriend. After that day when we welcomed Chang into our home, he was part of every gathering. We laughed at animal antics at the zoo, discussed cultures at museums, shared meals together regularly, discussed our differing faiths, and became lifetime friends. International friendship and missions came to our doorstep.

The book of Leviticus calls us to love the foreigner in our land simply because God is God. As His representatives, we share His love with all people, and in that sharing we are blessed.

God, You are Father to people from every land. Teach me to welcome all people just as You will one day welcome me into Your home in Heaven. And thank You for the opportunities for international friendship You provide. In Christ, amen.

Remember My Promises

I made a covenant with your forefathers when I brought them out of Egypt (Jeremiah 34:13).

Scripture: Jeremiah 34:8-17
Song: "Hail to the Lord's Anointed"

I sat by the phone, anxiously awaiting my CAT scan results. I was suffering from severe abdominal pain. When he called, the doctor explained that I had what appeared to be a solid mass on my pancreas. They were scheduling another test right away to take a closer look. My hands shook as I hung up the phone. Being a nurse, I knew what the doctor was thinking: cancer of the pancreas. We called our prayer warriors and waited.

As I lay on the table the day of the test, the Lord began to remind me of precious promises . . . that by His stripes I am healed, that He came to bring me hope and a future. Scriptures flooded my heart, and before going under anesthesia, I had peace.

The doctor was amazed at the results. A solid abscess had formed near my pancreas. Several days of antibiotics, and my health was restored. Our family was so thankful to God for His promises that day.

But news is not always good. Even in those times, God not only remembers His promises to us, but He is faithful to remind us of those promises, giving us a renewed sense of His presence and peace. In this way, too, He remembers His covenant.

Lord, thank You for bringing Your promises to us in our greatest times of need. Thank you for the peace they bring. With a grateful heart, I pray through Christ. Amen.

June 11–17. **Rhonda Thorson** lives in Oklahoma City, Oklahoma, where she serves as an academic advisor for Southern Nazarene University.

By the Way: He Still Restores

"Give your servant success today by granting him favor in the presence of this man." I was cupbearer to the king (Nehemiah 1:11).

Scripture: Nehemiah 1:5-11
Song: "Just as I Am"

As we pulled up to the driveway, I felt a lump in my throat. The house my parents had chosen to buy was a mess. It had yellowed, peeling wallpaper, stained carpet and torn tile, and standing water in the basement with dust and cobwebs everywhere. They saw the possibilities, I saw the mess. Though my parents each had their occupations, they enjoyed taking lifeless, neglected houses and restoring them to their original beauty.

And sure enough, soon the restoration was complete. The floors were covered with new carpet. Clean, fresh paint replaced the faded wallpaper and peeling tile. The water-filled basement was now a second kitchen and living area. People in the neighborhood were thrilled at the transformation.

Nehemiah received news of his people's plight. After returning from exile, the city was in ruins. The walls lay broken down, and the gates burned with fire. As Nehemiah prayed, he felt a call from God to do the work of restoration. Though he had an occupation—cupbearer to the king—he would return to God's people and begin restoring Jerusalem. God is still in the restoration business.

Lord, thank You for taking this lifeless, neglected house that is me and beginning a restoration. Continue to rebuild and restore me, teaching me to recognize opportunities to introduce others to your restoration business. Through Christ, amen.

Freedom in the Fishbowl

I will walk about in freedom, for I have sought out your precepts (Psalm 119:45).

Scripture: Psalm 119:41-48
Song: "Glorious Freedom"

All eyes stayed on a small goldfish sloshing around in a glass bowl as the youth pastor began speaking to the group. "Imagine the life of this poor goldfish. Trapped in this small space, he has no place to go. Living his life in total confinement, he has nothing to do but swim around in this little bowl, day after day. He will never get to experience the big world outside this bowl. In fact, I feel so bad for this goldfish I think I'll just set him free."

At that moment, he turned the bowl over and spilled the contents on the floor. The teens gasped as they watched the goldfish flop from side to side on dry ground. "He's free!" exclaimed the youth pastor. "No boundaries to keep him confined."

As he continued to talk, it was apparent the fish was dying. The youth pastor continued on with his sermon. Soon, a young girl in the youth group sprang to her feet, grabbed the fish and bowl, and rushed to a faucet to save its life.

As we search out the Lord's precepts, we can walk freely within His boundaries, knowing we are safe and secure. Just as fish were created to need water, we are created to need His guidance and care.

Lord, I thank You for Your precepts that keep me safe in times of danger, secure in times of insecurity, and certain of Your ways in a world of uncertainty. Help me to know the joyful freedom of following Your ways. In the name of the Father, the Son, and the Holy Spirit, I pray. Amen.

The Veil

Even to this day when Moses is read, a veil covers their hearts. But whenever anyone turns to the Lord, the veil is taken away (2 Corinthians 3:15, 16).

Scripture: 2 Corinthians 3:12-18
Song: "We Would See Jesus"

The candles are lit. The parents and grandparents are seated. The attendants take their places. The organ begins to play as the congregation rises. As the doors open, the long-awaited bride, draped in her satin white gown and clinging to her father's arm, walks down the aisle. As she passes, the congregation catches a glimpse of her face beyond a flowing veil.

At the end of the aisle stands the nervous groom. The dating, the planning, and the engagement have come to this moment. As the bride and groom join hands and face one another, the veil remains. Though thin and translucent, it prevents the bride and groom from freely looking into each other's eyes. Their view is distorted. But when the groom lifts the veil, he is able to gaze with delight at his beautiful bride.

Though not seen as often these days, traditional weddings bring to mind Christ and His church. And long ago the veils in the tabernacle, and in Solomon's temple, were in place to shield the most sacred things from the eyes of sinful man. But now, through Jesus Christ and His forgiveness, we are able to see the things of God without a veil to cover our hearts.

Precious Lord, I thank You for removing the veil from my heart and allowing me to see Your saving grace. Give me wisdom that can only come from You as I look to You in times of trial. In Jesus' name I pray. Amen.

Will He Do It?

He will keep you strong to the end, so that you will be blameless on the day of our Lord Jesus Christ (1 Corinthians 1:8).

Scripture: 1 Corinthians 8
Song: "God Is a Stronghold and a Tower"

Late night games, early morning prayer, 100 degree heat, bugs, lack of sleep, and awesome praise and worship—just a few of the ingredients that made up teen camp each year. My husband and I enjoyed directing the camp when we were in youth ministry.

As camp directors, we scheduled a meeting each morning of the week with our camp counselors. We'd update one another on the progress of camp, sharing joys, concerns, and special prayer needs. Afterwards, we'd spend time in prayer before waking up the campers to start a new day.

Day one was always exciting. The counselors came ready to tell of the amazing things God was already doing. By day three, counselors were late, sleepy, and growing weary. By the last morning, they were dazed and sunburned, wishing for a few more hours of sleep. Lack of sleep and constant physical activity had taken its toll. They were simply exhausted.

God promises that no matter how weak or tired we feel—no matter how great the temptation to throw in the towel in the final inning—He will keep us strong to the end. Can He do it? He is God. Will He do it? He promises.

Father, there are times in my life when I grow weary and feel my strength fading. Help me to stand on Your promises, especially then! In Christ's name I pray. Amen.

Just Do It

Do not merely listen to the word, and so deceive yourselves. Do what it says (James 1:22).

Scripture: James 1:19-27
Song: "O Word of God Incarnate"

But Lord, I argued, *how can I stop to help with this accident and leave my children in the car? There are other people around.*

There was a wedding in Cana. Jesus, His disciples, Mary were among the guests. Mary received word that they had run out of wine. This would be a terrible embarrassment to the family and an end to the great celebration. But Mary knew how to solve the problem; she first went to Jesus. Then she sought out the servants. "Do whatever He tells you," she said to the servants. They obeyed, and the first recorded miracle took place, as Jesus turned ordinary water into wine.

Do whatever He tells you. So I stopped at the accident scene. A young man had been thrown from his vehicle, and there were obvious signs of internal trauma. He had no pulse. Another bystander and I began CPR. The ambulance arrived.

We were never able to revive this young man. Did I save a life that day? No. Did I walk away, knowing I did what God had told me to do? Yes.

We don't always see or understand the outcome of our obedience. But we know we're to listen to the words of Mary spoken at the wedding, "Do whatever He tells you."

Lord, I thank You for that still, small voice that helps guide me each day. Give me ears to hear Your direction and leading, give me faith to obey, and give me eyes to see Your miracles as a result. In Jesus' name, amen.

Let the Bell Ring

In him we were also chosen, having been predestined according to the plan of him who works out everything in conformity with the purpose of his will (Ephesians 1:11).

Scripture: Leviticus 25:8-12, 25, 35-40, 47, 48, 55
Song: "Take Me As I Am"

The bell rang, and I looked up at the clock with dread. It was time for the class I would like to have skipped every day; the class that caused me to break out in a cold sweat; the class that had a way of humiliating me like no other class did: it was time for physical education. For some of my high school classmates, it meant demonstrating their great athletic ability. I was not athletic . . . or able.

Soon we would face the horrible ritual of choosing teams. Standing in a horizontal line like toys on display, the "captains" would walk up and down the line and choose the cream of the crop for their teams. Soon only a few of us remained. "Please don't pick me last" would race through my mind as I stood exposed for the poor athlete I was.

My self-esteem took a hard hit each time that bell rang. But these days I realize something marvelous: Scripture says God has redeemed me. I've been *chosen* for God's purposes. He is my Lord, and I was picked for His team. I'm not standing in the line wondering if I will be the last one chosen. I am bought, redeemed, chosen, called, and appointed by God himself.

Precious Lord, I thank You for choosing me and bringing me into Your great inheritance. I pray You will help me to uplift my fellow teammates and cheer them on to victory as we journey together. In Jesus' name, amen.

Mighty Miracles
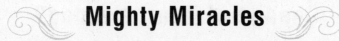

Give thanks to him who alone does mighty miracles (Psalm 136:4, *New Living Translation*).

Scripture: Psalm 136:1-9
Song: "Great Is Thy Faithfulness"

"Ever seen snow in June?" I recently asked my cousin Inell. She replied with a chuckle, "No, I can't say that I have."

Neither have I. However, I do know that, as today's Scripture verse mentions, God does mighty miracles. I am still in awe about the miracle He performed in helping me obtain a copy of a song I wrote over 43 years ago titled "Winter in June." I am happy to share this story in the month of June.

Having thrown away the two copies of "Winter in June" I had originally received from the company that had set it to piano music, I saw no way of getting another copy. Most people I discussed my idea with advised me to give up, because the company that published my song had gone out of business.

I didn't give up. I remembered and relied on Matthew 19:26, which reminded me that "with God all things are possible." I also followed the advice of a friend and contacted the U.S. Copyright Office. Sure enough, the company had registered my song! I attribute the quick response time to a mighty miracle from God as well. "Give thanks" . . . and I do.

Lord, thank You for this opportunity to write about Your faithfulness and love. I pray I never forget Your goodness. In the wonderful and powerful name of Jesus, amen.

June 18–24. **Jimmie Oliver Fleming**, of Chester, Virginia, says she is working hard and relying daily on Philippians 4:19.

Change of Heart Needed?

A man is not a Jew if he is only one outwardly, nor is circumcision merely outward and physical (Romans 2:28).

Scripture: Romans 2:25-29
Song: "Into My Heart"

When God established the circumcision covenant between Him and Abraham, it included specific requirements. "You are to undergo circumcision, and it will be a sign of the covenant between me and you" (Genesis 17:11). This would also apply to future generations. Every Jewish male would have to undergo the procedure at eight days of age—even the baby Jesus: "On the eighth day, when it was time to circumcise him, he was named Jesus, the name the angel had given him before he had been conceived" (Luke 2:21).

However, the act of circumcision alone could not fulfill all the requirements of the Jewish law, which the apostle Paul clearly pointed out (see v. 25). At the same time, since circumcision, according to Paul, is not merely "outward and physical," we can understand that a change must take place in the heart. This is the deeper requirement for fellowship with God, applying to both genders, whether for Jew or Gentile.

Do you need a change of heart toward a particular situation today? If so, remember Paul's words. Or as the prophet Jeremiah put it, prior to Paul's time: "Circumcise yourselves to the Lord, circumcise your hearts" (Jeremiah 4:4).

Lord God of All, help me to read Your Word with understanding. Open my heart to Your will, as You know me from the inside out. Help me to follow faithfully what I have learned. In the precious name of Jesus I pray. Amen.

Remembering Who We Are

What advantage, then, is there in being a Jew, or what value is there in circumcision? (Romans 3:1).

Scripture: Romans 3:1-9
Song: "A Charge to Keep I Have"

Can we always count on God's faithfulness? The apostle Paul answers the question in Romans 3. "First of all, they have been entrusted with the very words of God" (v. 2). However, some of the Jews were not faithful to the teachings of the Old Testament Scriptures. Yet this did not change God's faithfulness to them in any way.

Neither does it today when we fail. For as Paul reminds us in verse 9, "Jews and Gentiles alike are all under sin."

Still, as Christians, we have been entrusted with certain responsibilities. As a Christian writer, I have been entrusted on another level, as well.

When a friend recently sent me some of his writing to critique, he apparently thought I met the standard to "be entrusted." Ultimately, the choice would be his as to whether he would take my suggestions about his work, but he still valued my opinion. I felt honored to help my friend.

And while there are also certain advantages in having some expertise, I must be careful not to forget: the ultimate honor belongs to God. It was God who first entrusted me to work for Him as a writer.

Lord, thank You for my writing career. Help me to serve You in this capacity to the best of my ability. I want to be faithful to Your Word. It's my goal to pass it on in the same manner of faithfulness and truth. In Jesus' name, amen.

Hang In with Christ!

So then, brothers, stand firm and hold to the teachings we passed on to you, whether by word of mouth or by letter (2 Thessalonians 2:15).

Scripture: 2 Thessalonians 2:13-17
Song: "Standing on the Promises"

There's a song I like listening to on the radio that has these lyrics: "Sometimes you have to encourage yourself." I've often put this into practice. However, the most effective words of encouragement I've given myself first came from someone else. For example, while reading some letters I had written to myself recently, I saw that I had quoted Philippians 4:13 in both instances. "I can do everything through him who gives me strength."

The apostle Paul wrote these words, of course. And he certainly wrote many other words of encouragement in his letters. As indicated in the above Scripture verse, he encouraged the Thessalonica believers to stand firm. In the midst of their trials and physical persecutions, Paul's words were no doubt thankfully received.

We all need encouragement in our Christian walk. However, God calls us to *give* encouragement as well. And we can do so with our actions as well as our words. As someone once quipped: "A word of love is a work of love." Let us encourage someone today, like Paul, to "hang in there" with the Lord.

Heavenly Father, help me hold firmly to the faith You delivered to Your apostles. As I do, keep me ever thankful that You are my eternal hope and source of encouragement. In Your precious and holy name, amen.

Walk with Humility

He has showed you, O man, what is good. And what does the LORD require of you? To act justly and to love mercy and to walk humbly with your God (Micah 6:8).

Scripture: Micah 6:1-8
Song: "God Is So Good"

Although the frame from the inexpensive picture had cracked, I could still use the glass. This reminded me that, with God, we can never say: "All is lost." Actually, with God, *nothing* is ever lost. Nonetheless, it can be difficult to let this message register and live by it.

Still, God asks very little of us, even though He gives us His all. This has been so, starting with His only Son Jesus, who died on the cross for our sins, and up to this present day.

I want to open my eyes and really see this today. I'm trying to live the life I know God intends for me to live. He has not only shown me what is good, but has given me the good shepherd. What's more, I have this information in Jesus' own words: "I am the good shepherd; I know my sheep and my sheep know me" (John 10:14).

I am one of Jesus' sheep. And I've always viewed sheep as somehow having "humble" attitudes. In any case, that is what I want for myself. God has shown us what is good, and He wants us to "show" that we have received it by walking humbly with Him.

Heavenly Father, thank You for the privilege of being one of Your very own. Thank You for setting certain requirements and at the same time loving me unconditionally. I want to take Your hand and walk with You this day. In Jesus' name, amen.

Getting the Job Done

I saw what looked like a sea of glass mixed with fire and, standing beside the sea, those who had been victorious over the beast and his image and over the number of his name (Revelation 15:2).

Scripture: Revelation 15:1-4
Song: "Awesome God"

Something mysterious has happened to my computer. Its Date and Time function has reverted to the year 1996. Although I've tried, I haven't been able to successfully "reset" it to the current date. Thankfully, in spite of this problem, it still gets the job done.

However, after turning the computer on, I have to first hit the ESCAPE key before using it! The next step requires using a key to ENTER information about the computer system.

John, writer of Revelation, is said to have escaped to the Island of Patmos before entering certain information as well. Yet he got the job done. He wrote what God revealed to him to write. We can believe that he saw what he saw and that it means what it means.

In addition, we can visualize the scenes along with the apostle, which also involves getting the job done. For example, in Revelation 15:3, John writes, "Great and marvelous are your deeds, Lord God Almighty." What could be more pleasing to God than the job of being a witness to this every day of our lives?

O God, I often experience things that I can't describe or understand. Yet I know I should keep trusting You and Your Word. I know that in due time, You will open my mind to all the understanding I need. Through Christ I pray. Amen.

Reverencing God Today?

Fear the Lord your God and serve him. Hold fast to him and take your oaths in his name (Deuteronomy 10:20).

Scripture: Deuteronomy 10:12-22; 16:18-20
Song: "Change My Heart, O God"

I recently heard a sermon that truly made me stop and think. "God is the most heartbroken person there is," the minister declared. "And I'll tell you why. We don't fear God any more, or respect Him."

"You can judge by the way you answer these questions whether this applies to you," he added. "Do you serve Him like you should? Do you attend church as often as you should? Do you tell God you love Him?"

Admittedly, I could only answer "yes" to the second of the preacher's three questions. I do attend church as often as I should. With the other questions, however, I fall short.

Since the sermon made me stop and think, I will try to do better. Here's how: One, I can spend more time in a quiet time of prayer. Two, I can watch my language in private as well as in public. (I do tend to show disrespect by taking the Lord's name in vain sometimes.) And three, I can extend to God the kind of love I express with my children. Just as I freely—and often—express my love for them, I can also offer up my heartfelt love for God.

Lord, I love You. Forgive me for not saying it more often. Help me to give You more respect, as well. You've done things for me I can't name, so thanks for the second chance to express my loving thanks. As You so loved, please help me to do likewise. In the name of Jesus, amen.

What Would Jesus Do?

Again, when a wicked man turns away from his wickedness which he has committed and practices justice and righteousness, he will save his life (Ezekiel 18:27, *New American Standard Bible*).

Scripture: Ezekiel 18:25-32
Song: "Who Will Follow Jesus?"

You used to hear it quite often: "What would Jesus do?" While it seems to be a clever question—and one that can guide people when they're not sure what to do—it's only helpful if taken seriously. Research has shown that the Bible is the number one best seller in the world, yet the least often read. And we can see the perils of a people who refuse to read and digest the powerful Word of God: just watch the nightly news.

God wants us to live our lives in a "heavenly manner." That is, we're to live in ways that wouldn't seem out of place when we arrive there. And the Scriptures help us know how to do it.

I like how Meister Eckhart spoke of the practicality of simply living right in daily life: "To be right, a person must do one of two things: either he must learn to have God in his work and hold fast to him there, or he must give up his work altogether. . . . We must learn to keep God in everything we do, and whatever the job or place, keep on with him."

Almighty and everlasting God, help me to keep moving toward the glorious goal You have set—to become like Your Son, Jesus. In His name I pray. Amen.

June 25–30. **Le Lang** is currently serving as an elementary school counselor. She resides in Georgia with her husband and their two children.

Who Are You, in Faith?

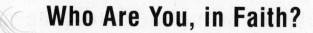

It came about in due time, after Hannah had conceived, that she gave birth to a son; and she named him Samuel, saying, "Because I have asked him of the LORD" (1 Samuel 1:20, *New American Standard Bible*).

Scripture: 1 Samuel 1:12-20
Song: "Spirit of Faith, Come Down"

The Bible tells us in Hebrews 11:6 that it is impossible to please God without faith. However, many people go through life without this most precious commodity. They don't seem to know the awesome power of God—or what He has in store for them, if they'll only stake their claim as His beloved children.

There is a reference to Jonathan's son Mephibosheth in 2 Samuel 4 and in 2 Samuel 9. His nurse took him and fled. While she was running with him, he fell from her arms and became lame. So the child grew up and was crippled in both feet. King David called for him, and he was given all the land of his grandfather, Saul. According to Scripture, Mephibosheth had very little to do with the blessing he received—accept for *who he was*.

Do you know who you are as a child of the Most High God? Do you believe that God blesses You in your obedience to Him? Hannah believed in God and had faith that He would answer her prayer. God did answer her prayer and allowed her to give birth to Samuel. What has your faith produced?

Dear Father, I sometimes forget that You have graciously called me to be Your child, adopting me into Your family. Thank You for Your willingness to see beyond my sin and unworthiness, to love me unconditionally. May I live in ways that make you proud! Through the precious name of Jesus, my Savior. Amen.

Great Faith and Obedience

The Lord visited Hannah; and she conceived and gave birth to three sons and two daughters. And the boy Samuel grew before the Lord (1 Samuel 2:21, *New American Standard Bible*).

Scripture: 1 Samuel 2:11-21
Song: "O, for a Faith that Will Not Shrink"

Imagine what Hannah must have felt like when God blessed her with five additional children. For so long she had been barren and wanted to have just one son. According to the Bible, she prayed and asked God to bless her with a child and promised to give the child back to God. She kept that promise, and God multiplied her blessing.

Of course, she *believed* God would answer her prayer. Have you ever asked God for something—and promised God that you would do something—if only He would give you what you asked for?

Parents often reward children for doing what they have been asked to do. And I enjoy doing something special for my children, especially when they have obeyed me. However, the rewards I give pale in comparison to what God does for His children.

Imagine how He feels when we obey Him. It must be a pleasure for Him to bless us, more and more. After all, He loved us enough to die for us!

O Lord, I am so thankful for Your willingness to hear my prayers and answer them with good things. Help me to come to You always with my deepest needs—not just to say what I think you want to hear, but to truly open my heart to You. In Christ, amen.

Here I Am

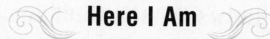

The Lord called Samuel again for the third time. And he arose and went to Eli and said, "Here I am, for you called me." Then Eli discerned that the Lord was calling the boy (1 Samuel 3:8, *New American Standard Bible*).

Scripture: 1 Samuel 3:1-14
Song: "Beautiful Witness"

Samuel was a young boy when the Lord called him three times. At first he thought Eli was calling him. He went and said, "Here I am." And Eli was mystified.

Have you ever felt a strong urge to do something good to help someone? Those could have been moments when God wanted to use you—was calling You just as surely as He called young Samuel. And did you listen to those promptings?

I've found that quite often my mind is so cluttered that it would be hard for me to recognize a gentle calling from God's Spirit. Yet I can recall times when struggling with a difficulty, some fellow believer has suggested a book for me to read or shared a passage of Scripture with me or simply said the encouraging words I needed to hear. Perhaps that person moved on God's prompting to take action!

Let us be ready to serve God and say, "Here I am, Lord, for You called me" (see v. 8). It is one thing to profess our love for God. It's quite another to be busy working for the Lord.

O Lord, remind me today of the great privilege it is to serve in Your kingdom work. Help me to find more times of silence, that I might be with You long enough to hear Your call. Guide me in using the gifts You've given me so that I can help others draw closer to Your salvation. In the name of Jesus I pray. Amen.

He Knows What's Best For Us

Samuel told him everything and hid nothing from him. And he said, "It is the LORD; let Him do what seems good to Him" (1 Samuel 3:18, *New American Standard Bible*).

Scripture: 1 Samuel 3:15–4:1a
Song: "I Hear Thy Welcome Voice"

When I was a girl, my mother made a lot of decisions for me. For example, there were times when I wanted to go somewhere, but she said no. Sometimes she'd share the reason for her decision; other times she'd give no explanation at all. The thing is, Mom had an uncanny ability to discern the good and the bad when it came to my friends.

I had what I thought was a good friend when I was in eighth grade. But Mom told me she really wasn't someone with whom I ought to spend a lot of time. Later I discovered that the friend was not only promiscuous, but she hung around older boys and did quite a bit of drinking. Mom had my best in mind.

God also has our best interests in mind, even when He may seem far away or hard to discern. But He is there for us, calling us to important work that we can accomplish through His strength. Here's how it worked for George Washington Carver: "When I was young, I said to God: 'Tell me the mystery of the universe.' But God answered, 'That knowledge is for Me alone.' So I said, 'God, tell me the mystery of the peanut.' Then God said, 'Well, George, that's more nearly your size.'"

Almighty God and Father, I am amazed to think that You care for me and have my best at heart. Guide me into the work You have for me to do in Your name, each day. May I please You always, in word and deed. In Jesus' name, amen.

Yes, He Will Answer

Moses and Aaron were among His priests, And Samuel was among those who called on His name; They called upon the LORD, and He answered them (Psalm 99:6, *New American Standard Bible*).

Scripture: Psalm 99
Song: "Did You Think to Pray?"

As a school counselor, I've met with many students who have been sent to me for disciplinary measures. For a while, those students would have to miss out on some of the activities enjoyed by their classmates. That is, they missed a blessing due to disobedience.

Can you imagine missing your blessing because you decided not to obey God? It would be such a pity for God not to answer us in our time of need. But does it really make sense for us to expect God to pour out blessings and answer us, when we live each day, saying and doing whatever we like? Surely that is unrealistic!

Yet God is merciful. Even as His Spirit is grieved, He reaches for us in love. He gently calls us to come back—and asks us to call sincerely upon His name.

He can do more than we can ever ask or think. Let us love and serve Him, not for the reward, but because we have come to so value the relationship with Him. Because we would hate to disappoint the one who has given us His all.

"Now to Him who is able to do immeasurably more than all we ask or imagine, according to his power that is at work within us, to him be glory in the church and in Christ Jesus throughout all generations, for ever and ever! Amen" (Ephesians 3:20, 21).

My Prayer Notes

DEVOTIONS®

JULY

Keep all my decrees and all my laws and follow them. I am the LORD.

—*Leviticus 19:37*

Gary Allen, Editor | **Margaret Williams,** Project Editor | Photo © iStockphoto®

DEVOTIONS® is published quarterly by Standard Publishing, Cincinnati, Ohio, www.standardpub.com. © 2011 by Standard Publishing. All rights reserved. Topics based on the Home Daily Bible Readings, International Sunday School Lessons. © 2008 by the Committee on the Uniform Series. Printed in the U.S.A. All Scripture quotations, unless otherwise indicated, are taken from the *HOLY BIBLE, NEW INTERNATIONAL VERSION®. NIV®.* Copyright © 1973, 1978, 1984 by Biblica Inc.™ Used by permission of Zondervan. All rights reserved. Where noted, Scripture quotations are from the following, used with permission of the copyright holders, all rights reserved: *King James Version (KJV),* public domain. *New American Standard Bible (NASB),* © The Lockman Foundation, 1960, 1962, 1963, 1968, 1971, 1972, 1973, 1975, 1977, 1995. *The Living Bible (TLB),* © 1971 by Tyndale House Publishers, Wheaton, IL.

How Do You Spend?

Then Samuel spoke to all the house of Israel, saying, "If you return to the LORD with all of your heart, remove the foreign gods and the Ashtaroth from among you and direct your hearts to the LORD and serve Him alone; and He will deliver you from the hand of the Philistines" (1 Samuel 7:3, *New American Standard Bible*).

Scripture: 1 Samuel 7:3-17
Song: "Unsearchable Riches"

What do we value these days? We're certainly accustomed to seeing fancy houses and cars. And shows on television often highlight the lifestyles of the rich and famous. Is it wrong?

Biblical personalities like Abraham, Isaac, and Jacob were rich and lived life abundantly. So being wealthy isn't necessarily bad, if we have our priorities in order.

On the other hand, problems can occur when our possessions begin to control us. Thankfully, the Scriptures are quite helpful here: "But store up for yourselves treasures in heaven, where moth and rust do not destroy, and where thieves do not break in and steal. For where your treasure is, there your heart will be also" (Matthew 6:20, 21).

So I ask myself today: What is my heart fixed on? Is it anything that could come between me and my love for God?

Father, let me rejoice in the goodness of Your creation and all the good gifts You give me. Help me to keep a thankfulness in my heart for the possessions You've loaned me for my time on earth. May I keep a loose grip on them! In Jesus' name, amen.

July 1. **Le Lang** is currently serving as an elementary school counselor. She resides in Georgia with her husband and their two children.

Respecting the Call

May the LORD now show you kindness and faithfulness, and I too will show you the same favor because you have done this (2 Samuel 2:6).

Scripture: 2 Samuel 2:1-7
Song: "Brothers, Joining Hand in Hand"

A few years ago, my husband and I left our church, in part because I disagreed with the church's choice of assistant minister. It would have been easy for me to harbor a completely unfavorable view of the small, struggling church of about 60 members. But my husband encouraged me to keep my negative feelings in check. While it was difficult to bite my tongue, I tried not to discourage others from visiting the church. In fact, I tried to trust that God had called this minister to the ministry for a reason—even if that reason was not to minister to *me*!

What I was upset about was minor compared to what David tolerated. After God chose David as king in place of Saul, Saul tried to kill him. David still honored Saul's position, even after Saul's jealousy became murderous rage (see 1 Samuel 19). He even honored those who buried Saul, the Lord's anointed.

God has placed a call on each of our lives. And while we don't always agree or get along, even in the body of Christ, we need to trust God's call on others' lives.

Dear Heavenly Father, help me respect other believers, even when I don't agree with them. Help me to see the gifts You have given others and appreciate them. I pray through Christ my Lord, amen.

July 2–8. **Lisa Earl** teaches online writing classes from her home in western Pennsylvania. She enjoys figure skating and spending time with her husband.

Shaking Things Up

The earth trembled and quaked, the foundations of the heavens shook; they trembled because he was angry (2 Samuel 22:8).

Scripture: 2 Samuel 22:8-20
Song: "Did You Feel the Mountains Tremble?"

Kool-Aid®, flannelgraph, pretzels, iced animal crackers, a picture of Jesus holding a wooly lamb in one hand and a staff in the other—such are my Sunday school memories.

Author Philip Yancey's Sunday school experience was much like mine. In his book titled *The Jesus I Never Knew*, he argues that, although Jesus is often portrayed as one-dimensional in the church and in popular culture, He is much more than "gentle Jesus, meek and mild." Jesus came to shake things up, and He overturned the religious establishment of His day.

Even His death was powerful. In fact so powerful that at the moment He died, the earth trembled, and the temple curtain that separated the Holy Place from the Holy of Holies was split in two (see Matthew 27:51). In the Old Testament only the high priest could enter the Holy of Holies, and even then under strict guidelines. When the curtain split, the need for such mediation was erased. Christ is now our mediator.

In today's passage God's wrath brought forth an earthquake. When Jesus died on the cross, God's wrath was satisfied with an earthquake. May Jesus shake up our lives today.

Jesus, thank You for moving Heaven and earth to bridge the gap between me and the God of the universe. Thank You for taking on my sin. Help me to show Your power in all I say and do. In Your name I pray. Amen.

Incoming!

You are my lamp, O LORD; the LORD turns my darkness into light (2 Samuel 22:29).

Scripture: 2 Samuel 22:26-31
Song: "The Light of the World Is Jesus"

At our community Fourth of July celebration, my husband and I sat behind a boy who was about 8-years-old.

"Incoming!" he shouted each time one of the fireworks went off. His announcements made people laugh at first, but his enthusiasm was eventually too much. The first few fireworks brought gasps from the rest of the crowd as well. But as we got several minutes into the show, everyone but the little boy quieted down and became complacent.

Jesus described himself as the light of the world—the one who came to turn darkness into light. This light is powerful! Today's passage reminds us that with God's help we can even "scale a wall."

How excited are we about His light? Are we prepared for His "incoming"? If we've been believers for a long time, have we allowed ourselves to become complacent?

While we don't need to literally shout about Jesus at all times, our actions can announce His "incoming." How we live our lives, how we treat others, and how we deal with conflict can all reflect His light. Let us reflect His explosive brilliance at all times and in all places.

Lord, help me to anticipate Your coming with joy and excitement. Allow me to maintain the joy of my salvation throughout my life. And let this enthusiasm be contagious to those around me. In the name of Jesus, amen.

Breaking Free

You broaden the path beneath me, so that my ankles do not turn (2 Samuel 22:37).

Scripture: 2 Samuel 22:32-37
Song: "Lead Us, O Father"

A few years ago I fulfilled a lifelong dream by taking figure skating lessons at my local rink. This may not seem like a huge accomplishment to many (it's not like I'm headed for the Olympics), but for me it was a breakthrough. Just stepping onto the ice and opening myself up to criticism was a leap of faith.

As a child I had to wear Forrest Gump–like braces on my legs, and I couldn't participate in sports. Even though I got to take the braces off in second grade, the stigma stuck with me through adulthood. It took me until I was in my mid-20s to have the confidence to get physically fit.

The knowledge that God promises to hold me securely has enabled me to conquer my fears. Psalm 121:3 says, "He will not let your foot slip—he who watches over you will not slumber." Similarly, today's passage promises that He will not let my ankles turn.

We all have "leg braces" in our past—things we need to trust God with, things that make it difficult to step into the slippery situations that life throws our way.

What can we surrender to Him today? No matter the struggle, God holds us in His hands.

Dear Father, free me from former struggles, even those insecurities I have carried since childhood. Help me to step out in faith to follow Your will for my life. Through Christ my Lord, amen.

Faithful Through the Generations

He gives his king great victories; he shows unfailing kindness to his anointed, to David and his descendants forever (2 Samuel 22:51).

Scripture: 2 Samuel 22:47-51
Song: "Faith of Our Fathers"

It's amazing how the faithfulness of one ancestor can change the lives of generations to come. My grandmother's parents were not churchgoers. Highly superstitious, they even visited German witch doctors to help "heal" severe burns my grandmother had incurred as a child. Although her parents didn't cling to God's promises, God had other plans for their daughter.

My grandmother began to attend church with a friend and was baptized as an adolescent. She married a Christian man and raised her children to know the Lord. She and my grandfather took my mom to church, and my parents in turn took me to church. I shudder to think how my life would be different if Grandma hadn't come to know Christ!

Because of God's covenant, we are all David's descendants. Jesus entered the world through the ancestral line of David, and through Him we are adopted as God's sons and daughters. The promise in today's Scripture holds true for us.

The decisions we make for our family will affect future generations. What a powerful incentive to follow God's ways!

Almighty and most merciful God, let me set an example for future generations by following You with my whole heart. Help me to lead others to You, that Your name would be blessed for all time. In the name of the Father, the Son, and the Holy Spirit, I pray. Amen.

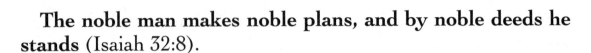

Laying It All Down

The noble man makes noble plans, and by noble deeds he stands (Isaiah 32:8).

Scripture: Isaiah 32:1-8
Song: "Draw Me Close"

I'm about to take a huge risk. It's a risk that our culture, financial experts, and even some churches would advise against. And quite frankly it scares me to death! I'm quitting my corporate job to stay home and take care of my coming baby.

Our household income will be reduced dramatically, and we will no longer have the security blanket of extra cash each month. I've been working full-time for 10 years, and the idea of losing control of my financial situation has me in a tizzy. Despite the risk, I feel called to care full-time for the son God has given us.

God's Word promises that when we plan faithfully, He provides for us faithfully. I need to trust that God will be faithful as my husband and I make what might be referred to as "noble plans."

We all have noble plans, don't we? Whether we're putting family before a career or putting God's standards ahead of peer pressure, we're trusting Him to guide us into the future. We can trust that He will allow us to stand firmly in His promises. Let us pray that we will be faithful in looking to Him for heavenly wisdom as we make our noble, earthly plans.

Heavenly Father, help me to make noble plans that will please and honor You. Help me to trust Your promises for my life and step out in faith, even when the future seems uncertain. I pray this through Christ my Lord. Amen.

Make No Mistake

The Spirit of the LORD spoke through me; his word was on my tongue (2 Samuel 23:2).

Scripture: 2 Samuel 23:1-7; 1 Chronicles 18:14
Song: "Shine for Jesus Where You Are"

When my grandfather died last year, we weren't sure if he knew the Lord. He never spoke of God, except to take His name in vain. He was a good man, a hard worker, and a respected business owner in his town. He attended church until his children were adults but not for the final 30 years of his life. When others spoke of Jesus, he got offended or changed the subject. His words were often laced with bitterness and criticism.

King David's last words were of the Lord. He spoke of God's covenant and was filled with God's Spirit. God even spoke through David, sprinkling his words with truth and grace.

I don't want my children to wonder about my commitment to Jesus. When I take my last breath, I want His words to be on my tongue. Words of hope, words of encouragement, words of faith and joy. I want His words to be on my lips and to shine through my actions, from the time my children take their first breath until I take my last.

Let us learn from David's example. Let there be no doubt about our commitment to Christ. Let us stand on Christ the solid rock, so that others will have no questions about who rules our hearts.

Dear God, I want to honor You until my dying day. Enable me to bless Your name with every breath I take. Help those around me to know that You are the Lord of my life. Thank You, in Jesus' name. Amen.

Resurrection Power!

That power is like the working of his mighty strength, which he exerted in Christ when he raised him from the dead and seated him at his right hand (Ephesians 1:19, 20).

Scripture: Ephesians 1:15-23
Song: "I Sing the Mighty Power of God"

Some years ago a newspaper conducted an interesting demonstration. A horse capable of pulling just over 9,000 pounds was paired with one that could pull slightly less than 8,000. Together they combined to pull an incredible 27,000 pounds! It's a principle called *synergy,* where the combined force or power exceeds the sum total of the power of the individuals involved.

There's something about strength combining with strength. Imagine God's strength combining with our own. How incredible is that? What are the possibilities?

Paul tells us the same power that raised Christ from the dead is available to you and me. Consider how this changes our perspective on what we can do in God's service. Don't we tend to limit our opportunities for ministry, focusing on our apparently inadequate abilities and resources?

Teach a class? Go on a mission trip? Who, me? We look within but fail to look above. Yet it's all about what God can do in and through us. It's synergy in action for His kingdom.

O God, the King of glory, open the eyes of my heart to the real possibilities for ministry based on Your power, looking beyond my limited capabilities. In Jesus' name I pray. Amen.

July 9–15 **Dan Nicksich** and wife Donna reside in Grant, Michigan, where Dan serves as the senior minister of the Northland Church of Christ.

Well, the Bible Says . . .

The mouth of the righteous man utters wisdom, and his tongue speaks what is just. The law of his God is in his heart; his feet do not slip (Psalm 37:30, 31).

Scripture: Psalm 37:27-34
Song: "Wonderful Words of Life"

I began attending a Christian church during a time of crises in my life. I didn't know the Bible but I was rapidly learning. I can still recall conversations with numerous people in the church and their consistent responses to my questions. Some of them were leaders or Bible teachers, but others were simply Christians. And yet my numerous questions were always met with the same reply, "Well, the Bible says . . ."

David says that righteous wisdom and words flow from the heart of one who has the law of God planted deep within. Yet we don't often spend time meditating on God's Word. Our fast-paced world doesn't allow time for what is perceived as passive, perhaps unproductive pursuits. But Scripture repeatedly extols the power and virtue of time spent in godly reflection.

Wait for the Lord? Our action-oriented culture cries out for more. The law of God in one's heart? Why bother? I've got seven translations on my computer.

But today, please join me in spending some time in meditation upon the Word of God. Let us seek heavenly treasures hidden from view, available to all who approach with an open heart.

Dear Father, help me to plant Your Word deep within my heart. May it be a reservoir of strength, compassion, and virtue in times of need. In the holy name of Jesus, my Lord and Savior, I pray. Amen.

I Will Go to Him!

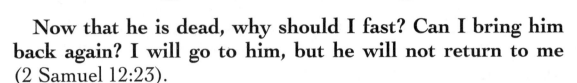

Now that he is dead, why should I fast? Can I bring him back again? I will go to him, but he will not return to me (2 Samuel 12:23).

Scripture: 2 Samuel 12:20-25
Song: "A Rest Remaineth for the Weary"

On Saturday, Harry buried his wife of 48 years. On Sunday, he was in church to worship. A number of people expressed surprise upon seeing him there.

"Where else would I be?" he asked. "Where else would I be except in God's house, with God's people, praising the Lord with my church family? Marge and I were always here, and God is still the same; He's worthy of my praise."

King David had just lost a child. For seven days, he had fasted and prayed, pleading for the child's life. But the child died.

David's response is memorable: he prepared himself for worship. Following his time with God, he ended his fast. Worship precedes feasting, and for David it even superseded the most intense grieving.

Many seem to find a reason to turn from God in the loss of a loved one. David's determination was to live in such a way so as to someday be reunited with his departed son. "I will go to him, but he will not return to me." I would like to live as David did in this regard: as one looking forward to a reunion with loved ones who have gone before.

O Father, how inspiring are those who trust in a time of grief! Help me to learn from their example. Deepen my trust, be my security, strengthen my faith. In the name of Your Son, my Savior, I pray. Amen.

The Son Who Would Be King

Solomon your son shall be king after me, and he will sit on my throne in my place (1 Kings 1:30).

Scripture: 1 Kings 1:28-37
Song: "O Father, Bless the Children"

When our youngest son completed his first year of Bible college, he asked if he could preach in my place on his first Sunday home. "Can you believe it?" I quipped to a friend. "You send your son to Bible college and, first thing you know, he wants to take your job!"

I can't imagine how David felt when one of his sons had rebelled and tried to take his throne. David survived that attempt, but now another son was seeking to set himself up as king despite Dad's choice of another. David took decisive action to ensure that his chosen successor, Solomon, would rule.

It's always exciting when children follow in our footsteps. David must have been thrilled to have a son worthy of his throne. Your children may not rule empires, but they need to know they have your approval.

Do your children know how you feel about them? I've presided over too many funerals where children lamented the fact that Dad had always "struggled to express his feelings." Some were still struggling over a perceived lack of approval. So be sure there is no room for doubt in the minds of your children. Let them know how you feel about them before it's too late.

Father, You have told us that children are a gift from Your hand. Help me to appreciate and nurture these precious gifts so that our love for them and You would always shine through. I pray in Jesus' name. Amen.

Dependent on Grace

Adonijah, in fear of Solomon, went and took hold of the horns of the altar (1 Kings 1:50).

Scripture: 1 Kings 1:41-53
Song: "Father of Everlasting Grace"

I was a teenager when President Nixon resigned from office. It may have been the clearest example of the old saying, "Power tends to corrupt, and absolute power corrupts absolutely." Richard Nixon's desire to hold onto power led him down a road of corruption and to a place of disgrace.

Adonijah sought power, and he wasn't above seeking it through corrupt means. He mistook David's age for weakness, his illness for lack of resolve. But now the plot had unraveled, and his would-be supporters quickly deserted him. He was reduced to a man holding onto the horns of the sacrificial altar in a desperate plea for his life. He wanted to be king but now he's a pathetic figure, totally reliant on the grace and mercy of the true king.

It's hard to feel sympathy for someone like Adonijah. We mistakenly brand the sins of others as so much worse than ours. But I find that the picture of him desperately holding on to the altar serves as a precious reminder. What am I in God's sight except someone desperately hoping for God's mercy? Take no delight in the disgrace and downfall of another, for we are all like Adonijah, totally dependent on the king's grace.

Lord, may I never take pleasure in the misfortune of others. Help me to remember Your amazing grace and be more concerned that others would come to know of the forgiveness awaiting them, as well. In Jesus' name, amen.

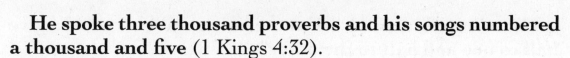

Lasting Wisdom

He spoke three thousand proverbs and his songs numbered a thousand and five (1 Kings 4:32).

Scripture: 1 Kings 4:29-34
Song: "Eternal Wisdom, Thee We Praise"

I can imagine Solomon's sons on the playground. Instead of, "My dad's stronger than your dad," they could say, "My dad's wiser than your dad," and who could argue?

Wiser than who? Scripture affirms that Solomon's wisdom exceeded that of Ethan the Ezrahite, Heman, Calcol, and Darda. While these might have been well-known names in Solomon's day, his is the only name that merits attention today.

And consider his productivity: 3,000 proverbs and 1,005 songs. In a curious twist, one of Solomon's more philosophical pieces of literature (Ecclesiastes 3:1-11) was used as the basis for a hit pop song about 3,000 years later. While Solomon penned the words, it was The Byrds who set them to music. The songwriter donated 45% of the royalties to an Israeli cause since he acknowledged that his lyrical contribution was limited to six words and the title, "Turn, Turn, Turn." Other than that, it's all Solomon.

Kings sent advisers to Solomon to seek his advice. But you don't have to journey to a distant land to hear wisdom from the king. In a legacy that stretches back for centuries, Solomon continues to be a source of guidance, strength, and wisdom.

Lord, I subject myself to unnecessary hardship and pain whenever I ignore Your words of guidance. May Your wisdom become that which guides, directs, and strengthens me through each day. In Christ's precious name, amen.

Decisions

He then gave an order: "Cut the living child in two and give half to one and half to the other" (1 Kings 3:25).

Scripture: 1 Kings 3:16-28; 2 Chronicles 9:8
Song: "They Will Know We Are Christians by Our Love"

A man watched his wife's car plunge into a river. She made it out of the car but was struggling to keep her head above the icy water. He realized he had but moments to make an agonizing decision: save his wife or try and save his teenage son who was still trapped in the car.

It's hard to imagine such a heart-wrenching decision. How does one differentiate between love for a spouse and love for a child?

Solomon was counting on the love of a mother when he rendered his decision. Only a mother would willingly give away her son in order to save his life. All Israel held Solomon in high esteem for the wisdom he displayed in his ruling. Indeed, foreign dignitaries journeyed from near and far in order to personally experience and better appreciate Solomon's gift of wisdom. And they truly saw it as a gift from God.

God places each of us in situations and circumstances where we can make a difference. Whether to the grieving, the lost, the weary, I pray that others would recognize God working in and through you, just as they did Solomon. What a blessing when God is praised because of how we live for Him!

Father Almighty, may others see Christ in me. May it always be that His blessings would inspire praise, not for me, but for You. In the name of Jesus, who lives and reigns with You and the Holy Spirit, one God, now and forever, amen.

The Blessing of Receiving

He longed to fill his stomach with the pods that the pigs were eating, but no one gave him anything (Luke 15:16).

Scripture: Luke 15:11-24
Song: "Blest Be the Tie That Binds"

DO NOT PREACH ON THE PRODIGAL SON. I found that command in bold print on a rescue mission pulpit. Visiting preachers wore out that theme on the mission congregations, whose main interests were food and shelter. But I've preached on the Prodigal many times elsewhere. Yet I never thought to mention that poignant phrase, "No one gave him anything."

We can envision the lost son buying drinks for the crowd—party guys do that. They give to win friends. But when the money ran out and he found himself destitute and desperate, no one gave the young man anything. What a contrast with our experience as Christians!

We are giving people, saying, "It is more blessed to give than to receive" (Acts 20:35). But receiving brings blessing too. While we do not give to be repaid, our portfolio of love pays unfailing dividends.

A certain pride nudges us to be self-sufficient, to resist help, perhaps robbing friends of the blessing of giving. But receiving is a humbling, enriching experience, and we must not shun part of the love that binds us to each other. How blessed we are when God's love through friends brightens a dark moment.

Thank You, **Lord,** for the times when friends came alongside to help me. Thank You for allowing me to become part of a caring fellowship. Through Christ I pray. Amen.

July 16–22. **Lloyd Mattson** is a retired minister, editor, and writer who divides his time between Duluth, Minnesota, and Tucson, Arizona.

Down with Gloom and Doom

Sing to God, sing praise to his name, extol him who rides on the clouds—his name is the LORD—and rejoice before him (Psalm 68:4).

Scripture: Psalm 68:1-6
Song: "Joyful, Joyful, We Adore Thee"

Let's leave the pity party. Things are bad, I know, but things have always been bad. The world has known no good old days since Eden lost its luster. Jesus came to bring light. Yes, we are called to concern and compassion, but we are also called to joy.

Joy fills the Bible, because joy lies at the heart of the gospel message. So we Christians walk through life with a confident smile, knowing Him in whose presence we find fullness of joy.

On the day of this writing, I heard stories by elders in a remote Alaskan village, stories of incredible hardship, heartache, fear, and death. Yet the elders smiled, remembering the day they found Jesus. Religion had taught them about Christmas and Easter, historical truths; a missionary taught them that Jesus walks with His followers day by day.

I visited the cemetery behind the mission chapel. Tangled grass and alder hid old graves. White, wooden crosses sagged, their legends long faded. A small plot held bones from an ancient burial ground eroded by the tide. Unknown, said the small crosses.

But to be known of God! That's joy unspeakable.

Thank You, **Lord,** for joy, even when I cry. I cannot help but be sad for hurting people around me, but I have a good word for them. Help me to radiate Your love and share your joy. In the name of Jesus, amen.

Nickel and Dime-ing God?

All these people gave their gifts out of their wealth; but she out of her poverty put in all she had to live on (Luke 21:4).

Scripture: Luke 20:45–21:4
Song: "Take My Life and Let It Be"

The story is told of an evangelist famed for his offering appeals. One evening he said, "Tonight I don't want to see folding money in the collection plate; just your pocket change. All of it." Amazingly, the offering was considerably above average. The people literally nickel-and-dimed God, with quarters and half-dollars thrown in. The evangelist understood the giving habits typical of congregations.

Money is a touchy subject, and church leaders employ all manner of devices to work around that. Some suggest if we just give enough, God will make us rich. But giving to get isn't giving, it's gambling. Scripture does not hint that the temple widow who gave her mite got rich—she already was rich. The value she placed on her faith proved that.

Nothing more clearly reflects our values than our checkbook. We tout the tithe as the biblical norm for giving, but that's risky. The test lies in what we do with the ninety percent. Some say only what we give to the church and missions counts, but caring for our families and helping the needy around us is also giving to God. The widow had it right: She gave her life to God, and money was part of the package.

Thank You, **Lord,** for the abundance You have supplied—enough to meet my every need. Help me learn that the value of money lies in the good it can do for others. Through Christ, my Lord and Savior I pray. Amen.

Piety or Just Mashed Potatoes?

One day Elisha went to Shunem. And a well-to-do woman was there, who urged him to stay for a meal (2 Kings 4:8).

Scripture: 2 Kings 4:8-17
Song: "Make Me a Blessing"

Word came that Carol had died, a friend of 60 years. She and her husband, Harold, hosted me graciously on many occasions over the years, but my thoughts went back to the Holm farm where Carol grew up.

I was serving my second charge, a small church in a northern mining community. My salary never quite reached around. We had four young children, all of us living in an old parsonage with no insulation and a hungry furnace. Thirty below was not uncommon. Elsie's genius with hamburger creations served us well, but how I coveted invitations for Sunday dinner! Given our large family, invitations were few, except from the Holms.

Many Sundays found us at their table enjoying pot roast, brown gravy, snow-white mashed potatoes from their garden, and homemade apple pie. Sometimes we even went home with a freshly beheaded chicken. The Holms were Christian but not overtly religious. Yet they clearly possessed the gift of hospitality. (I'll take mashed potatoes over piety any day.)

Adding six plates to an already full table was inconvenient. But the family showed love to their young pastor, and that's what I remember. Elisha remembered a home-cooked meal. If you want to be remembered, be a hospitable friend.

Lord, grant me the grace to be a cup of cold water to friends all around me, whether or not it is convenient for me. Through Christ, amen.

Mission Accomplished

She went up and laid him on the bed of the man of God (2 Kings 4:21).

Scripture: 2 Kings 4:18-27
Song: "Oh, Come, Little Children"

When we've got kids to take care of, safety comes first. We drive carefully and keep a wary eye out for strangers. We monitor games, rescuing shy kids from playful bullies.

Kids are keen observers. They sense genuine interest and crave individual attention. A kid's most memorable moment may be telling a story to an adult who really listened. Adults who "live Jesus" are more important to kids than those who simply talk about Him.

One summer a group of us flew into a remote Ojibwa village to build a mission house. Village men watched with cool indifference, lifting no hand to help. Teens tried to appear indifferent, but their interest was evident, mischief in their eyes. Mothers watched warily, uncertain about these strangers. But the children, lots of them, jumped in with boisterous enthusiasm. They remained underfoot though the week, often a nuisance.

As the work progressed, we wondered what impact we were making; there were no opportunities for gospel meetings. But at the end of week, as we made our way to the planes, a child spoke this benediction: "You men are kind to kids." Mission accomplished.

Help me, **Lord,** to remember what it was like to be a child—how I longed for adult attention and affection. Let me give myself to children in my community and church. Help me be kind to kids, in the name of my Savior. Amen.

The Power of Personal Contact

As he stretched himself out upon him, the boy's body grew warm (2 Kings 4:34).

Scripture: 2 Kings 4:28-37
Song: "We Are One in the Bond of Love"

A person stricken with hypothermia has only one hope for survival: the immediate application of external warmth—a preheated cover or a warm, sustained embrace. Covering the victim with heaps of blankets does no good; the victim's capacity for generating internal heat is gone.

When we're hurting, we usually don't need advice; we need love and understanding. A minister whose wife was dying of a long illness said, "If one more person offers to pray with me, I think I will punch him out."

Was that man crass, cold, unspiritual? Those who have been there will understand. He needed a pat on the shoulder, the squeeze of the hand, a hug that says I care, someone to stand by. Does the Bible hold more pathos-laden words than Matthew 26:40? "Could you men not keep watch with me for one hour?"

When friends hurt, pray from a distance, hug up close. Sustaining one another is the whole idea of the church, the fellowship. Too often our focus on outreach overrides in-reach. We need to bring our lives close to one another and to strangers who may wander in. People long for peace and warmth. It's cold out there.

Heavenly Father, keep me close to those who need me. Let the love of Christ be my counsel. Open my heart to the young and aged, and love them through me. In the name of Christ I pray. Amen.

Obedience and Prudence

The woman proceeded to do as the man of God said (2 Kings 8:2).

Scripture: 2 Kings 8:1-6
Song: "Be Thou My Vision"

The confidential directive from the home office reached the manager's desk. She had gained her position through loyalty, creativity, and hard work. Prosperity followed, and the future looked bright for this Christian woman.

The directive dismayed her. Though veiled in tangled "legaleeze," its requirements were ethically marginal, probably illegal. Though she might not be held personally accountable, she could not in good conscience comply. So she faced a tough decision. The kids were heading for college. The family was used to a comfortable lifestyle. And there was a sizable mortgage. Good jobs were scarce, and finding one at her present income was all but impossible. Nevertheless, she cleaned out her desk.

No, she didn't get a better job. Family plans had to be restructured and a more economical home found. Relationships suffered strain. Friends thought she had lost her mind. All that the woman gained was a heart right with God. There is no peace like the peace of obedience.

Prosperity does not always follow obedience, but the new values gained never depreciate, and God promises to meet all our needs. (Who really needs a mansion, anyway?)

Father in Heaven, grant me the grace to obey Your Word, regardless of critics or cost. Teach me true values and grant me the sense of peace that obedience brings. In the name of Your Son, my Savior, I pray. Amen.

Who Says?

The Lord is our Judge, our Lawgiver and our King; he will care for us and save us (Isaiah 33:22, *The Living Bible*).

Scripture: Isaiah 33:13-22
Song: "Praise to the Lord, the Almighty"

"You gotta do it," 6-year-old Laura screeched at her younger brother. "Now!"

"Who says?"

"Mommy says."

"*She* didn't tell me," her brother challenged.

"Well *I'm* telling you. You gotta listen to me."

"Do not!"

"Do so!"

They may have come to blows if I hadn't intervened yet again. The truth is, Laura takes her role as big sister seriously. She can be very bossy. It's probably a good thing that her brother is learning not to allow her to push him around. Still, I can't help but wonder what they will be like as adults.

In families and the workplace it's not uncommon to find someone who likes to play the big boss, whether or not they have earned it. Is there an answer? Yes, but only in surrendering what we believe is our "right" to be the boss — and in submitting to the one who is Lord of all — will we find peace with others.

Lord, You know how often I try to control what others say and do. You also know the times when I even try to tell You what to do. Please forgive me. Teach me the joy of allowing You to be Lord, surrendering to Your perfect will. In Jesus' name, amen.

July 23–29. **Marlene Bagnull** is a wife, mom, and grandmom. She has published eight books and directs the Greater Philadelphia and Colorado Christian Writers Conferences.

Hand-Me-Downs

He will defend the afflicted among the people and save the children of the needy (Psalm 72:4).

Scripture: Psalm 72:1-7
Song: "The Wonder of It All"

"Stop being so wasteful," my mother constantly scolded me when I was little. She'd holler when I left the light on in my bedroom and when I didn't eat every bit of food on my plate. And she saved everything! I remember the kitchen drawer where she kept pieces of string that she rolled up in little balls.

What I hated the most were the hand-me-down clothes I had to wear. I didn't understand why there was never money to buy me a new dress. The kids in school made fun of me for the clothes I wore and for being poor.

It's no wonder I grew up feeling like a second-class citizen. "It's not fair!" I'd complain to my mother. "I don't like being poor. Why can't I have things other kids have?"

Mom didn't have any answers.

For many years I carried a big chip on my shoulders and struggled with low self-esteem. But then, in the Book that has been handed down from generation to generation, I discovered how much I matter to God. He values me not for what I own but for who I am. Not only that, He promises to provide for me. My complaining has changed to praise for His unfailing love.

Lord, thank You for loving me and for the opportunities You give me to hand my faith down to the next generation. May my children and grandchildren revere You. May we together sing Your praises. In the precious name of Jesus, amen.

Breaking the Law

Happy are all who perfectly follow the laws of God (Psalm 119:1, *The Living Bible*).

Scripture: Psalm 119:1-8
Song: "Follow Me, the Master Said"

My heart started pounding when I saw the police car with lights flashing through my rearview mirror. Quickly I pulled over.

"You just went through that stop sign," the officer said.

"I'm so sorry," I said. "Honestly, I didn't see it."

"You're going to tell me you also didn't see the speed limit sign?" he replied.

"Oops. I guess I was a few miles over the limit. But I wasn't speeding. I just didn't want to be late picking up my daughter from play practice. She worries when I'm not there on time."

"I'm sure she does," he said. "But if you don't slow down, you won't get there at all."

"I really am sorry. I've never gotten a ticket. And we're really struggling to pay our bills . . ." By now I was close to tears. The officer gave me a stern warning but not the ticket I deserved.

God has given us His laws so we are without excuse when we end up willfully disobeying them. The fact is our lives and the lives of those around us will be much happier when we follow the laws God has established rather than our own desires. After all, like stop signs, they are for our own good.

Lord God, I confess I am often like a stubborn child. I do what I want to do and then try to justify my actions or make excuses. My joy is lost until I confess my sin. Thank You for Your laws that teach me how to live for You. In Jesus' name, amen.

Know-It-All

This is what he says to all mankind: "Look, to fear the Lord is true wisdom; to forsake evil is real understanding" (Job 28:28, *The Living Bible*).

Scripture: Job: 28:20-28
Song: "Change My Heart, O God"

"Don't even try to show her how to do it," my coworker warned me. "She's such a know-it-all you'll never convince her you've got a better way to get the job done. You'll only end up frustrating yourself."

"But she's wasting so much time," I said.

"And you'll waste even more of your time—and hers—if you try to get her to change her way of doing things."

I sighed an irritated and exasperated sigh. No doubt we've all met a know-it-all. We may work with one or live with one. That can be really tough. If you're like me, it's not easy to keep your mouth shut when you know you have a better way.

I need to remind myself to extend grace to the know-it-all who annoys me. After all, there is enough of the know-it-all in my own nature. How often do I ask God to bless what I've made up my mind to do?

And then there are the times when I can subtly fall into the world's way of thinking about my values. Then may I remember that the fear of the Lord is true wisdom.

Dear Heavenly Father, please forgive the know-it-all in me. Forgive my arrogance. Give me a heart that seeks after You in all things, along with a humble spirit that acknowledges You as the source of all wisdom. Work in me to make me more like Your Son, Jesus. In His name I pray. Amen.

Help!

O our God, won't you stop them? We have no way to protect ourselves against this mighty army. We don't know what to do, but we are looking to you (2 Chronicles 20:12, *The Living Bible*).

Scripture: 2 Chronicles 20:5-15
Song: "The Battle Belongs to the Lord"

Great Britain was a mighty empire. She was not about to give up her colonies in the New World because some rebels had declared independence. And so the battle began. Ships carrying the best trained army in the world sailed for America. The Continental Army was hardly a match, yet against all odds they prevailed and won the war for independence.

Oftentimes the odds do seem stacked against us. Life's circumstances may cause us to feel overwhelmed and helpless. Our boss may give us a huge assignment with a deadline that is impossible for us to meet. Worse still, we may have lost our job and given up hope of finding something else. The bank may be threatening to foreclose on our home. Or we may be facing a serious crisis in our family for which we have no answers.

"O Lord, help! We don't know what do."

No matter the size of the problem, God is never overwhelmed or surprised. Although He may not fix it the way we think it should be fixed, we can be certain that He will not abandon us. As we look to Him, He will help us to go through each trial.

Lord, You know my frustration when I feel backed into a corner by a seemingly impossible situation. You know how hard I try to fix things on my own. Forgive my stubbornness. Help me to learn to turn to You more quickly. In Jesus' name, amen.

A Holy Boldness

He boldly followed the paths of God—even knocking down the heathen altars on the hills, and destroying the Asherim idols (2 Chronicles 17:6, *The Living Bible*).

Scripture: 2 Chronicles 17:1-6
Song: "Once to Every Man and Nation"

"Stand up! Sit down! Fight! Fight! Fight!"

I remember yelling those words at the top of my lungs at many a football game when I was in high school. I'd pump my fist in the air and cheer until I was hoarse. And then there were the pep rallies the day before a big game. How could they not win with our cheers urging our players on to victory? Unfortunately there were still many heartbreaking losses—and no state championship for my alma mater—despite the bold moves our guys made on the field.

Boldness should not be reserved only for sports. Indeed, God calls us to take a bold stand for Him in a culture that increasingly seeks to silence Christians. Will we have the courage to take on today's issues, confronting evil with good, and doing what Jesus would do?

It won't be easy to proclaim the gospel in the days ahead. But it never has been easy. At least, to this point, most of us can agree with Hebrews 12:4: "In your struggle against sin, you have not yet resisted to the point of shedding your blood." Thank God, but let us prepare, boldly, no matter what comes.

Lord God, please forgive me for the times when I have been silent. Give me a holy boldness to speak Your truth in love. Help me not to miss any opportunity to share the difference You will make in our lives, if we only believe. In Jesus' name, amen.

Honest Hearts

These were his instructions to them: "You are to act always in the fear of God, with honest hearts" (2 Chronicles 19:9, *The Living Bible*).

Scripture: 2 Chronicles 19:4-11
Song: "I Would Be True"

"You could just tell your mother that we'll be studying at my house," Sharon said.

"And not tell her that boys are going to be there?" I asked.

"Come on. You don't need to tell her everything, do you? Besides what she doesn't know won't hurt her."

"But you know my mother," I insisted. "She has a way of finding out things I don't want her to know. She seems to have a sixth sense that makes her keep asking when I'm not telling her the whole truth."

Sharon rolled her eyes. "You're just afraid to make up a story."

That was true. I was afraid. I had gotten caught in a lie once, and the consequences weren't pleasant. What pain when I heard the disappointment in my mother's voice! "I don't know that I can trust you anymore," she had said.

Peer pressure isn't just for teens. We all face the temptation to compromise the truth with the excuse that "everyone else is doing it." The fear of getting caught will never be enough to keep us honest. Only the fear of the Lord—and a deep desire not to disappoint Him—will give us honest hearts.

Thank You, **Lord,** for what I learned from my mother about the importance of honesty. Help me never to compromise the truth, despite what others do. Instead, may I honor You through an honest heart and truthful lips. In Jesus' name, amen.

Breaking Faith

So guard yourself in your spirit, and do not break faith (Malachi 2:16).

Scripture: Malachi 2:10-17
Song: "More Holiness Give Me"

"'I hate divorce,' says the Lord God of Israel" (Malachi 2:16). Those words burned in me like molten metal as I struggled with the charred remnants of a 16-year-marriage. Not even for the sake of my children was I willing to continue in a relationship that had become toxic for both of us. I could barely manage to commit to the dissolution; there was no way in the world that I could pretend it was OK.

In spite of having preached fervently against divorce, I found myself at a lawyer's office. I could talk about years of scorn and sarcasm, about the disrespect and contempt. But ultimately, it was our mutual failure to "guard ourselves" in our spirits that led to the breach of faith between us.

I would come to know the agony of separation from my children—the loss of closeness that I had treasured with them. Yes, I learned pain.

But I also learned grace. Facing my own failures, I finally embraced the grace that flows, even for those who have done that which the Lord hates. He forgives because He is unwilling to break faith with those to whom He has promised salvation.

Dear Lord, may we never abuse Your grace as an excuse for breaking faith with our spouse, our family, our friends, and especially with You. In Jesus' name, amen.

July 30. **Doc Arnett** and his wife of 20 years, Randa, live in St. Joseph, Missouri. They both work at Highland Community College in Kansas.

An Eternal Dominion

His dominion is an eternal dominion; his kingdom endures from generation to generation (Daniel 4:34).

Scripture: Daniel 4:34-37
Song: "Yesterday, Today, Forever"

After my father died last summer, two of my brothers and I were looking through the tools and carpentry "junk" he'd accumulated in his basement. Back in one cabinet, on the bottom shelf, was an old Rockwell drill. It was heavy, massive, even the casing was made of steel. Dad had bought the drill to use when building a livestock barn back in the year I was born, 1953.

It was the first power tool I'd used. Barely strong enough to lift it, I bored holes through pieces of scrap wood, marveling at the chips and shavings flying out from around the bit. Nearly 60 years later, the drill still works. Even though the bearings have taken a beating over the years and the motor has lost some of its torque, it still works.

We marvel at things that endure: good tools, ancient buildings, strong marriages. Of how much greater wonder, then, is a kingdom, invisible and powerful, begun nearly 2,000 years ago, which will still endure 10,000 years from now?! And it will still be working.

No wonder that Jesus taught His disciples that those who are least in the kingdom are greater than the greatest of those who are outside the kingdom.

Lord, we give You praise for Your power and dominion, we give You praise for the kingdom that You have established, for the kingdom that will endure forever. And we thank You for granting us faith that we might enter that kingdom. Amen.

DEVOTIONS®

AUGUST

The LORD reigns forever, your God, O Zion, for all generations. Praise the LORD.

—Psalm 146:10

Gary Allen, Editor | **Margaret Williams,** Project Editor   Photo © iStockphoto®

The Illusion of Seeking God

[They] seem eager for God to come near them (Isaiah 58:2).

Scripture: Isaiah 58:1-9b
Song: "I Want to Be a Worker for the Lord"

When I was a kid growing up on a dairy farm in Kentucky, I loved baseball. I'd fantasize about playing in the majors. Using an old bat, I'd pick up rocks from the driveway and knock them into the cow lot. "There's a deep ball to right center field!" the announcer in my head would exult. "It's going back, back, way back. This one's going right out of here, ladies and gentlemen."

I'd go through the entire batting order of the St. Louis Cardinals, driving in run after run. I'd spend hours, too, throwing a baseball up on the tin roof of the stock barn and catching it when it came rolling down off the shed. Even when I was walking through the pasture or the hayfield, I'd still be fantasizing about baseball, swinging an imaginary bat at the alfalfa blooms or fescue stems. What I didn't do was spend a lot of time *practicing* baseball. I didn't put in the long hours of strength training, real batting practice, and working on fielding skills. There was too much pretending . . . too little doing.

While God takes pleasure in the prayers and praises of His people, He surely delights in seeing our lives speak deeply of our devotion through active compassion, hospitality, and mercy.

Almighty and gracious Father, help me to truly glorify You in worship and in my service to You by ministering to others. In the name of Jesus, Lord and Savior of all, I pray. Amen.

August 1–5. **Doc Arnett** and his wife of 20 years, Randa, live in St. Joseph, Missouri. They both work at Highland Community College in Kansas.

The Reality of Finding God

The LORD will guide you always; he will satisfy your needs in a sun-scorched land (Isaiah 58:11).

Scripture: Isaiah 58:9c-14
Song: "As the Deer Pants for the Water"

When we bought this house, the outside was a wreck. The word *neglect* in an illustrated dictionary must have displayed a picture of our yard. A mass of tangled vines grew right up against the backdoor steps. Weeds ranged alongside the house. A mass of dead branches and old leaves matted the ground beneath the trees. And the entire yard tilted toward the house, channeling rainwater right into the basement.

With a rented bucket loader, I created a relatively flat croquet area, sloped slightly away from the house. Randa helped me set the base stones of a new retaining wall. We also worked together to clear away the old tangle. Then while I set about building the wall, she began the gardening part of our landscaping.

Three years later, a lush mix of shade plants thrives under her care. Huge hostas spread beneath the walnut and maple trees. A mix of ferns, bleeding hearts, lilies, and a dozen other varieties flourish in our beautiful backyard. Each day, I admire Randa's work—and the change it has brought to this place.

Such is the change that God promises to us when we dedicate ourselves to honoring Him and being Christ's loving hands and feet in the world.

God my Father, bless us in our labor for You, in our love for others, and in our striving for justice for the poor and oppressed of this world. In the name of the Father, the Son, and the Holy Spirit, I pray. Amen.

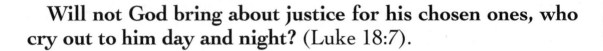

Go for the Red Jersey

Will not God bring about justice for his chosen ones, who cry out to him day and night? (Luke 18:7).

Scripture: Luke 18:1-8
Song: "Jesus Shall Reign"

I was pretty much the runt of my small eighth-grade class at Trenton Elementary School back in the early 60's. But I loved basketball, and I was used to the hard work of a row-crop and dairy farm. And since I'd earned some playing time on our "varsity" team as a sixth-grader—and had been a starter in the seventh grade—I'd assumed I'd be a starter in my eighth grade year. Our new principal and coach made no such assumption.

Mr. Tribble had me wearing a yellow jersey during our practice scrimmages. (The red jerseys were reserved for the prospective starters.) Instead of sulking, griping to my parents, or filing a petition with the school board to have him fired, I played as if every scrimmage was a championship game. I rebounded, scrapped on defense, and scrambled for loose balls as if someone were trying to take away my inheritance. By the end of the second week of practice, I was wearing a red jersey, and I kept it throughout the entire season.

Our persistence and determination often matter more than our size or our ability. When it comes to righteous justice for the "least of these brothers of mine" (Matthew 25:40), there's never an excuse for being content to wear a yellow jersey.

My Lord and Savior, let me never grow weary in doing good, and especially in doing good for others. Help me persevere, regardless of the things that may fight against me. In the name of Jesus, amen.

Justice to Workers

You trample on the poor and force him to give you grain (Amos 5:11).

Scripture: Amos 5:8-15
Song: "How Sweet, How Heavenly Is the Sight"

My brother-in-law is a talented trim carpenter. Whenever he finishes a job, there will be no gaps or cracks showing in the joints. A couple of years ago, he invited Randa and me to come look at the house in which he was installing trim.

It was some house! Multi-levels, arched doorways, elaborate entryway, curving staircase and on and on. It seemed ostentatious to me, but I've been sheltered from a lot of material excess.

While we were taking our tour, I noticed a few other men working. When I asked Kevin about them, he said, "They're painters. They work for the guy who's building this house. They aren't union, but he's got them doing carpentry work anyway."

I wondered what it would be like to build a mansion for someone who had made his fortune by bidding jobs at union scale and paying his workers the bare minimum that would keep them working. To me, making them do this work was an additional insult.

It is a natural fact that most people will do whatever they have to do in order to feed themselves and their families. When entrepreneurship exploits that, reaping the benefits of others' labor without sharing the fruits, it verges into sin.

Help me, **Father,** to remember that justice begins with how we treat one another, especially when we occupy the advantaged position. In the name of Your Son, my Savior, I pray. Amen.

Goals Greater Than Wealth

He upholds the cause of the oppressed and gives food to the hungry (Psalm 146:7).

Scripture: Psalm 146
Song: "We Give Thee but Thine Own"

"This is the 'Year of Double,'" a preacher announced in 2002. "The Lord is going to double everything you give this year. Whatever you give, He'll give back to you twice as much." A couple we know believed the message and donated five thousand dollars. That wouldn't be a lot for some people, but I knew that their combined annual salary at the time was quite low.

I see a disturbing trend in the American church: increasingly, influential preachers seem to promote a "gospel of prosperity." Church members share stories of gain and promotion rather than stories of enduring tribulation and overcoming the world.

"So, did the Lord double your money?" I asked the couple. "No," the husband answered, "not that we could ever see."

"So what did you do?"

Without pause, he looked me in the eye and answered, "We remembered that we gave the money to help spread the gospel in India. I don't think the Lord wanted to shortchange us with material returns. There will be souls in Heaven that wouldn't be there if we hadn't given the money."

"Anything else?" I probed.

"Yes," he grinned. "We found another church."

Lord, help us to remember that it is more blessed to give than to receive—and that the trying of our souls refines our faith. Help us to make justice for others a goal greater than achieving wealth for ourselves. In Jesus' name, amen.

Watch the Signs

When Pharaoh saw that the rain and hail and thunder had stopped, he sinned again: He and his officials hardened their hearts (Exodus 9:34).

Scripture: Exodus 9:27-35
Song: "O Come Before the Lord"

The story goes like this: A man was sitting at home when he heard a flash flood report. But instead of evacuating, he stayed home. As water poured into his house, he climbed onto his table.

A friend came by in a little boat and offered to take him to dry land, but he refused. As the water continued to rise, the man climbed into his attic. Another friend came by in a larger boat to rescue him, but he still refused. Finally, the rushing waters forced him to climb onto his roof. So a helicopter dropped a ladder to him to pull him to safety. But you guessed it—he refused.

After being swept away in the floodwaters, he perished in the storm. Then he asked the Lord, "Why did You let me die in the flood?" Of course, God shook His head and said, "I sent you two boats and a helicopter!"

It's amazing how many times we look past the signs God places before us as we move along life's journey. Pharaoh hardened his heart as he ignored the Lord's warnings, but we don't have to close our eyes to God's merciful messages.

Lord, I confess I've not always paid attention to the signs You've placed before me. I know You love me, Father. So I ask You to give me wisdom to see how You're leading me—and a soft heart that is pliable in Your hands. In Christ's name I pray. Amen.

August 6–12. **Pete Charpentier** serves as a minister in Hammond, Louisiana. He is also the author of a book on mentoring others in spiritual growth.

Regrets and Redemption

What has happened to us is a result of our evil deeds and our great guilt, and yet, our God, you have punished us less than our sins have deserved (Ezra 9:13).

Scripture: Ezra 9:10-15
Song: "Have Mercy, Lord, on Me"

When my wife and I were engaged, I made a huge mistake. Due to certain circumstances, I decided not to buy her an engagement ring. I never realized how deeply I hurt her in that moment. In fact, we didn't experience God's complete healing until we had been married for 16 years.

One of the truths I learned during those years was that God's grace really is unconditional. You see, I had always prided myself with trying to live without regrets. But I had the awful regret of scarring my wife, whom I loved more than anything. Yet, I couldn't fix the mistake because I couldn't turn back the hands of time. So God used my wife's unconditional love to be the clearest expression of His grace I've ever encountered.

All of Scripture focuses on God's redemption, and we see this surface in Ezra 9:10-15. Although Israel had returned from exile, she was still imperfect and had to deal with the consequences of her sin. But the Bible is a long book because God is long-suffering. We are punished less than our sins deserve, but it's not because the Lord is unjust. It's because He's gracious.

Almighty and most merciful God, I thank You for not treating me as my sins deserve. Your grace is truly amazing. I praise You for sending Your Son to take my sin upon himself so I can experience Your free gift of eternal life in Him. I pray this prayer in the name of Jesus, my merciful Savior and Lord. Amen.

God's GPS

But if you do not obey the LORD, and if you rebel against his commands, his hand will be against you, as it was against your fathers (1 Samuel 12:15).

Scripture: 1 Samuel 12:6-16
Song: "Wherever He Leads I'll Go"

In the summer of 2008, I traveled from Mississippi to my uncle's funeral in south Louisiana. Instead of listening to a friend's advice and following the interstate, I decided to use my GPS and take the scenic route. That was a mistake.

After maneuvering through twists and turns and navigating across a river on a ferryboat, I faced my biggest challenge. The road I was traveling turned from pavement to gravel to dirt. But my GPS kept prompting me to "veer left." The problem was that a levee was on my left! So after backtracking, stopping for directions, and being told to drive on the levee, I decided to do it and finally arrived at my destination.

Sometimes we find ourselves in "new territory," just as the Israelites did in our Scripture reading. They never had a king before. Still, God was telling them that if they followed the lead of His Word, things would go well. But if they disobeyed His lead, they would have problems.

While obeying God's Word doesn't mean life will be easy, it does mean life will work. The Scripture is like the Lord's "GPS" —God's Positioning Scripture—directing us on our journey.

Lord, Your Word tells me to trust You more than my own understanding. And I am called to acknowledge You in all my ways, thus You'll direct my path. Today, I look to You for direction. Help me to follow Your Word. In Jesus' name, amen.

More Than a Name

If we claim to have fellowship with him yet walk in the darkness, we lie and do not live by the truth (1 John 1:6).

Scripture: 1 John 1:5-9
Song: "Living for Jesus"

Few people know my full name, and fewer know the story behind it. I'm named after my French great-grandfather, Pierre Charpentier. I'm told my grandfather wanted my mother to name her son after his dad, but when my oldest brother was born, she forgot. She promised my grandfather she would name her *next* son Pierre. But when my other brother was born, she forgot again. So my mother swore to name her *next* son Pierre.

And then I came along. This is why my full name translated into French is Pierre Pierre Charpentier, or in English, it's Peter Peter Carpenter. I guess my mother was so focused on my first name that she never thought of a middle name. But most people don't call me Pierre anyway. They call me Pete. Yet they know who I belong to because of the family resemblance.

How about people who claim the name "Christian"? A name is a good thing, but a person needs more than a name. He or she needs a family resemblance. John tells us that if we only make a claim—or only have a name—it's not enough. We also need to live by the truth. That way, everyone can see the family resemblance we share with our heavenly Father.

My Lord God, I want to thank You for saving me and giving me the name "Christian" as Your child. Please help me to represent the name well so everyone can see a family resemblance between You and me. In the name of Jesus, who lives and reigns with You and the Holy Spirit, one God, now and forever, amen.

Finish Strong

I have fought the good fight, I have finished the race, I have kept the faith (2 Timothy 4:7).

Scripture: 2 Timothy 4:1-8
Song: "The Fight Is On"

The Queen's Baton Relay is a powerfully symbolic opening to the Commonwealth games. Everything begins at Buckingham Palace as the queen places her "message" into a special baton and hands it off to an honorary runner. The race then proceeds like a relay, as one person passes the baton off to another.

Over the years, the Queen's Baton Relay has grown. Today it spans literally thousands of miles, over several months, and touches over 70 nations. The final runner returns the baton to the queen at Buckingham Palace, who removes her message and reads it to announce the official beginning of the games.

You know, every Christian is a part of the king's relay. The baton is the gospel, and the track is the whole world. This baton has passed through hands like those of the apostle Paul, who ran his leg of the race faithfully and finished strong. It has been carried in the hands of believers like Polycarp, Wycliffe, and Luther. Now the king's message is in our hands. May we run faithfully until the day we kneel before Jesus and hear Him proclaim His message: "Well done, good and faithful servant!" (Matthew 25:21, 23). Then the celebration of eternity will begin.

Lord God, I'm humbled at the thought of carrying Your message to the world. Thank You for all the faithful witnesses who have run before me, and please give me the strength to run my race well and finish strong for Your glory. Through Christ, amen.

Shine—in Words and Works

I am the light of the world. Whoever follows me will never walk in darkness, but will have the light of life (John 8:12).

Scripture: John 8:12-19
Song: "Lead, Kindly Light"

As the congregation gathered in their church, no one was prepared for what was about to happen. Minutes before the evening service started, the lights in the church winked, and then stayed off. Since the people were already gathered and the ministry team was in place, the minister called for the service to continue as planned.

Of course, the guest speaker used this situation to make one of his main points. As he stood preaching in the dark, he reminded the members of the congregation to reflect Christ's light throughout their community and beyond.

Jesus clearly calls His followers to let their light shine and not to hide it under a bowl (see Matthew 5:14-16). Yet many Christians are sitting silently in the shadows instead of shining Christ's light! So perhaps the most powerful sermon preached that night wasn't in the minister's words but in the thick darkness hanging in the air.

In our Scripture passage, Jesus proclaims himself to be the light of the world. As we reflect His light, we offer others the opportunity to receive eternal life in Him. Let's not hide His light but let it shine through our words and our works.

Lord Jesus, You are the light of the world, and I thank You for calling me to reflect Your light. Please give me wisdom and boldness to shine Your light so everyone can see and believe the truth of the gospel. In Jesus' name I humbly pray. Amen.

Wonderful Savior!

He will be called Wonderful Counselor, Mighty God, Everlasting Father, Prince of Peace (Isaiah 9:6).

Scripture: Isaiah 9:1-7
Song: "There's Something About That Name"

I love the classic movie *It's a Wonderful Life* because it shows how Heaven's view of life is different from earth's view. You'll remember that as the story begins, two angels are discussing George Bailey's life. Of course, if you've seen the movie, you know George Bailey is about to end his life because he's discouraged. But Heaven knows George's life is a wonderful life. Contrary to even his opinion, his life isn't one of waste but significance. (Again, how Heaven views a life and how the earth views the same life are often very different.)

While the original words of Isaiah 9:1-7 were given in the days of King Ahaz, the ultimate fulfillment of this prophecy is found in Jesus. But can you imagine the night Jesus was born? Mary is a Jewish girl pregnant out of wedlock, and Joseph is a humble carpenter. Both of them have no place to go. Yet the child born that night is the sinless Son of God. He isn't merely the offspring of Mary and Joseph, He is God, wrapped in flesh. Although earth rejected Him, He is Heaven's perfect gift to save us. And now Jesus reigns at God's right hand. His life is unparalleled. It's truly a wonderful life.

Lord Jesus, You are matchless in Your majesty. Words can't adequately describe You. Everything I need I find perfectly met in You alone. You're my Wonderful Counselor, Mighty God, Everlasting Father, and Prince of Peace. I worship You in spirit and in truth. In Your name I pray to the Father. Amen.

Fighting Freddy

Fight the good fight of the faith . . . keep this command without spot or blame until the appearing of our Lord Jesus Christ (1 Timothy 6:12, 14).

Scripture: 1 Timothy 6:11-16
Song: "Onward, Christian Soldiers"

Freddy punched me in the face and snarled, "Meet me after school, unless you're chicken." Our music teacher, Mr. Collins, distracted by a room of noisy eighth-grade boys, didn't notice. And when class ended, Freddy, a big kid, sneered and sauntered off. Fight or run? I worried for the rest of the school day.

"Fight the good fight of faith" thunders down through the ages, ordering Christians to strap on the "full armor of God" (Ephesians 6:11) and engage the enemy. Believers are "to keep this command" until relieved of duty when Christ returns.

There's Freddy! I groaned, spotting him and his cronies in the park. I forced myself toward the battlefield. A spectator ring formed, and Freddy and I clashed. Remembering my dad's boxing lessons, I landed a jab or two and dodged his lunging attack. Then, suddenly, it was over—a draw. For me, the real struggle, more than the fight itself, was the decision to face my foe.

Deciding to battle evil takes courage, because fighting for God is risky. Yet believers obey, for the ultimate victory is His.

O gracious God, I report for duty this day, wanting to serve You. Please give me the courage to fight the good fight. In the name of Christ, I pray. Amen.

August 13–19. **Wayne Pearson,** living in Hutchinson, Kansas, is a retired worship minister and public school music teacher.

Checkpoint Heaven

How great is the love the Father has lavished on us, that we should be called children of God! (1 John 3:1).

Scripture: 1 John 2:28–3:3
Song: "Jesus Loves Me"

"What's your license?" demanded the burly uniformed officer. Confused, I hesitated. His penetrating gaze fixed on me while I fumbled for an answer. There was no reason for my nervousness as my wife and I handed our passports to the agent. Certainly, no contraband lurked in our luggage. Only the happy memories of a family reunion in the majestic Canadian Rockies traveled with us.

"License?" I mumbled. Then I understood. "Oh, my license plate. We're from Kansas." He nodded and passed back our documents. "Welcome home!" he added and waved us through the Alberta/Montana border checkpoint.

Welcome home! Back in my country—my birthplace, I mused. It felt good to be back in the USA. However, my valued American citizenship is only temporary. Someday, I'll arrive at checkpoint Heaven. In a flight of imagination, I envision a radiant angelic agent who greets me and asks, "What's your name?"

Dazzled, I whisper my name.

The figure smiles and says, "Just a moment," and opens the Lamb's book of life. "Here it is. You're the adopted son of the Heavenly Father. *Welcome home!*"

O Eternal Lord God, thank You for accepting me into Your family and giving me a heavenly inheritance. I love You, because You first loved me! All praise to You, in the name of Your Son, Jesus! Amen.

Wind Gauge

He that troubleth his own house shall inherit the wind (Proverbs 11:29, *King James Version*).

Scripture: Proverbs 11:27-31
Song: "It Is Well with My Soul"

"Look!" I laughed and stopped the car for my wife to see. There, placed by the good-humored folks of Rolla, Kansas, was a sign—"Western Kansas Wind Gauge." Bolted to the center of a sunflower design was a hefty logger's chain. Along the edge of the sunflower, from the bottom up to 90 degrees, were labeled markings: "calm (unheard of in Western Kansas)," "gentle breeze," "kite-flying weather," "shifting sand," "stand clear of flying links," and finally, "tornado stopper." Wind strength was gauged by the position of the chain. Kansans, especially, get the humor. However, fierce windstorms are not funny to tornado alley folks. Sometimes, onto the high plains roaring twisters will snake down from monster thunderheads to rip, maim, and kill. Recovery from the massive destruction is tough. Some victims never do. Weather services issue tornado warnings when funnel clouds are sighted. Sirens scream danger, alerting those in the storm's path to take cover.

Weather alerts are also issued by God. For example, Scripture warns that anyone who "troubleth his own house shall inherit the wind." To avert any sin twister threatening our homes, we must heed the Lord's warnings and seek shelter in Him.

Lord, You shelter us in times of trouble and danger. Thank You for protecting us. In Jesus' name we pray. Amen.

What's in a Name?

No longer will violence be heard in your land, nor ruin or destruction within your borders, but you will call your walls Salvation and gates Praise (Isaiah 60:18).

Scripture: Isaiah 60:17-22
Song: "Jesus Is the Sweetest Name I Know"

"Wayne," the conference speaker said to me over the loud-speakers. "Your name means 'wagon.'" The two thousand gathered in the convention hall—mostly Christians—chuckled. Not me. I was thunderstruck. A new conviction of my sins had surfaced at this conference, so I was already troubled. In fact, I was miserable. *Now this!* I whimpered. *God was scolding me by name.*

The Lord's message seemed clear to me: "Wayne, you're a Christian, so act like one. Wagons carry heavy loads."

The teacher continued: "Your name also means to help others who are weighed down with problems—to be a bearer of burdens."

My wise mother-in-law once gave me a handwritten list of God's names, along with their Scripture references. On it "Salvation" was included. Certainly, "Jesus" means "to save" (see Matthew 1:21), and saving us is His primary purpose. Even so, as I read Isaiah 60:18 I wonder, *Why name walls?*

Then I realized that God is my wall of salvation. In Him, I am safe and secure. When I stray, He will call me back home—even by name at a conference.

Blessed Lord, You are my salvation and my wall of protection. I am safe and secure in Your care for me, every day of my life. Therefore may my entire life bring praise to Your name. Through Christ, I pray. Amen.

Heart Song

Sing to him a new song; play skillfully, and shout for joy (Psalm 33:3).

Scripture: Psalm 33:1-5
Song: "Jesus Paid It All"

How awful! Horrible! I shuttered and, with the others in the audience, watched in stunned silence as the speaker, without another word, walked from the pulpit to sit at the grand piano. I anticipated great teaching when I attended the "Mind of Christ" seminar led by T. W. Hunt—seminary professor, church musician and, most important to me, my respected friend.

Through Dr. Hunt God blessed me, surpassing by far all my expectations. Throughout the seminar, he quoted Scripture by heart, adding insightful comments about the customs of the time. Then, without sensationalism, he revealed the details of our Lord's horrible suffering.

To think that Jesus endured such agony for me overwhelmed my emotions and boggled my mind. Knowing the awful details of His ordeal is shocking; however, that knowledge fills me with gratitude. How amazing that, willingly, Jesus took my beating and endured my execution. I shout for joy—sometimes aloud and sometimes silently within—cheering the Lord's bravery.

That night, my teacher, brother-in-Christ, and friend, played an old hymn. But as I listened, my grateful heart sang a new song: "Jesus paid it all, All to Him I owe."

Heavenly Father, forever I will sing Your praises and glory in the cross of Your Son. I am so thankful that He atoned for me there, leaving the riches of Heaven to take on human nature. In Jesus' name, I pray. Amen.

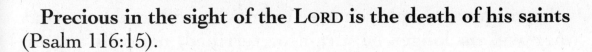

Lemons in Heaven

Precious in the sight of the LORD is the death of his saints (Psalm 116:15).

Scripture: Psalm 116:5-19
Song: "Face to Face"

"Why is there a lemon tree?" 4-year-old Mallorie asked her dad as we three strolled through their home church. "A lemon tree?" my son Matthew responded. She pointed toward a sculpture attached to the hallway wall. "Oh, that's a memorial," her daddy said as they stepped back to look at the polished wood trunk and branches. "It helps us remember special people who went to church here. Their names are printed on these bronze leaves that—oh, I see—they look like lemons." Mallorie considered the tree for a moment and then said, "Someday, I want to be a lemon too."

All Christians want to be a lemon someday. We hope that our efforts to serve the Lord and bless others, are remembered. My own dad, who died recently, was a "lemon." "Arnold" isn't embossed on a bronze leaf or listed on a plaque. Yet his generosity, his fun-loving humor, patience, faith in Jesus, service to the church, and deep love for his family memorialize him in the hearts of those who knew him. He was a precious man. And to know that he is also "precious in the sight of the Lord" is joy, indeed. I'll see him again . . . with all the other lemons!

Almighty and gracious Father, thank You for preparing a heavenly home for me. Help me tell others of the eternal blessings You have for all those who trust You. And may my own legacy—the things I've done and said in my lifetime—bring You honor. I pray this prayer in the name of Jesus, my Savior and Lord. Amen.

Needy Sheep

"I will place shepherds over them who will tend them and they will no longer be afraid or terrified, nor will any be missing," declares the LORD (Jeremiah 23:4).

Scripture: Jeremiah 23:1-6; 33:14-18
Song: "Savior, Like a Shepherd Lead Us

Bone chilling rain, sleet, and snow pelted David and me. He yelled over the wind. "Hang on! I've got to get the mommy on her feet."

"OK!" I shouted as I clutched the hind feet of a mucky, blood-smeared just-born lamb. All this was new and thrilling to me—a wide-eyed city kid. Soon, we shepherded the ewe and carried the lamb from the prairie to the barn close to David's farm home. There in the shelter the sheep rejoined the flock. *How needy sheep are*, I thought.

To God, we are sheep-like. True, we are "wonderfully made" (see Psalm 139:14)—tough, intelligent, and creative. Even so, we need God, the shepherd, and other people, the flock. Of course, the Lord knows this and, because He loves us, provides for our needs. His greatest provision was Jesus, the good shepherd. Through Him and the Holy Spirit, eternal blessings are ours.

Also God gives us one another. We are called to love each other in word and deed. In this way to, as we care for our brothers and sisters in Christ, we are shepherded by the Lord.

Lord, thank You that you are the good shepherd. I know that, regardless of my failings and troubles, You will always carry and shelter me as I journey through life's storms. You protect and care for me. And when I die, You "restore my soul." I pray, rejoicing in Jesus' name. Amen.

No Need to Be Afraid

Yea, though I walk through the valley of the shadow of death, I will fear no evil; For You are with me (Psalm 23:4, *New King James Version*).

Scripture: Psalm 23
Song: "You'll Never Walk Alone"

Three times a week Joe and Emily followed the same routine. He'd get out of bed to help her wash and dress. Then Joe would drive Emily to the hospital for another painful treatment to battle her deadly disease. Married for 50 years, they'd experienced many hard times. But in the last several months, Emily had become more dependent on Joe for her care.

Never once did she hear him utter a word of complaint. Instead, Joe was always at her side to encourage her, wipe her tears, and help her in any way he could. No matter how difficult the situation, Joe constantly lavished acts of love on his dear wife. She took comfort in knowing he'd stay close to the end.

Jesus promised He'd never leave us alone. By coming to live on earth, He experienced human suffering, rejection, loneliness, and the kinds of trials we face. That's why David wrote that he would "fear no evil"; he knew God was always with him, for his comfort. We have that same assurance. Whatever we may face today, God is with us and wraps us in His love.

O God, You already know what I will face today, and You have promised to never leave me alone. So whatever lies ahead, I will not be afraid. I am secure in knowing You are by my side, and I rest in Your presence. In Jesus' name I pray. Amen.

August 20–26. **Jeffrey Friend** is a writer and speaker living in Largo, Florida. He is a certified professional in Human Resources and a die-hard fan of the Baltimore Orioles.

Somebody's Watching Me!

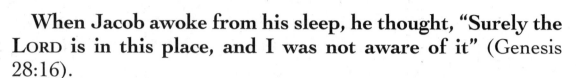

When Jacob awoke from his sleep, he thought, "Surely the LORD is in this place, and I was not aware of it" (Genesis 28:16).

Scripture: Genesis 28:10-17
Song: "Surely the Presence of the Lord"

For months the boss had suspected Tom of stealing products from the loading dock, so he decided one afternoon to go into a remote area of the warehouse where he could watch Tom as he worked. It wasn't long before the boss noticed that, as Tom worked by himself unloading the trucks, he would occasionally place a box in a darkened area close to the loading dock. At the end of his shift, Tom backed up his pickup to a side door and began loading it with the boxes he had set aside.

When the boss suddenly appeared and told Tom he'd been watching him for a few hours, Tom only said, "You were right there the whole time, and I never even knew it."

The Bible abounds with stories that remind us that God is always watching us. Nothing we do escapes His eyes. He is pleased when He sees us following and obeying Him, but He also knows when we do not. In our darkest moments or in our greatest joy, He is always present. Let us be aware that our Father constantly watches over us. And let us take comfort in knowing, as Jacob did, that we are never separated from His love and care.

O God, as I go through my day, sometimes I'm not aware of Your presence. But You are constantly watching over me. You protect and care for me every moment, and You lavish me with Your love. Thank You for all Your blessings! Through Christ, amen.

But I Want It My Way!

Joseph was upset when he saw that his father placed his right hand on Ephraim's head. So Joseph lifted it to move it from Ephraim's head to Manasseh's head (Genesis 48:17, *New Living Translation*).

Scripture: Genesis 48:17-21
Song: "Have Thine Own Way, Lord"

Harry had interviewed for the supervisor position two weeks ago, and he knew this was the day the manager's decision was to be announced. Shortly before lunchtime, the news came that Luke had been selected. Harry angrily confronted the manager and shouted, "That job should have been mine! I've been here for over 20 years, and Luke has only been here a few years. I work hard every day and know the business inside and out! How could you pick Luke? How could you make such a mistake? You chose the wrong man!"

The manager explained, "I know you think you should be the new supervisor. But I did make the right decision. I looked at all the facts and considered all angles. You may not believe it, but I do know what I'm doing, and my decision stands."

Joseph became upset when his father did not bless the first-born son. He even tried to interfere and move his father's hand, although his father knew exactly what he was doing. Like Harry, Joseph only had his own selfish motives in mind. We need to trust God's decisions and actions, accepting that He knows—and desires—what is best for us.

Dearest Lord, help me to overcome my selfish desires and seek Your will in my life. Thank You for forgiving me when I complain when things don't go my way. May I pray like Jesus, "Not my will, but yours be done" (Luke 22:42). In His precious name, amen.

"You Can't Be Serious, God!"

Moses said to God, "Who am I, that I should go to Pharaoh and bring the Israelites out of Egypt?" (Exodus 3:11).

Scripture: Exodus 3:9-15
Song: "There Were Twelve Disciples"

Only four minutes remained, and the home team needed two touchdowns to win. But now the starting quarterback was writhing in pain on the field. The coach looked at the second-string quarterback and said, "OK, Jones. It's all up to you. Get in there and lead this team to a win!"

"But, Coach, I haven't played all year! I don't have enough experience, and the team will just ignore me. I know I'll mess everything up and be ridiculed."

The coach looked him right in the eyes and said, "Jones, I am counting on you to rally this team. If you get in that huddle and anybody complains or disrespects you, then you just tell them that I am the one who sent you in and put you in charge. Then step up and be the leader we need right now."

Like Jones, Moses also knew what it was like to be called to do an assignment he thought he wasn't prepared to do. But God assured Moses: My authority is all the support you'll need.

We may sometimes feel unworthy or unqualified to do God's work. But He will always provide the strength and guidance we need to succeed.

Precious Father, sometimes I feel unworthy or unqualified to serve You. But throughout the generations You have always used flawed people to fulfill Your plans. Help me overlook my own shortcomings and focus on Your strength and wisdom. In the name of Jesus, Lord and Savior of all, I pray. Amen.

Think Before You Act

This is what the LORD Almighty says: "Give careful thought to your ways" (Haggai 1:7).

Scripture: Haggai 1:7-14
Song: "Stop, Poor Sinner, Stop and Think"

As John hung his head and stared at the floor of his jail cell, his mind flooded with memories from the past several years. He recalled the many times his parents had pleaded with him to be careful when choosing his friends. They'd urged him to stay away from places where trouble lurked and asked him to choose to "do the right thing," even when it was difficult.

But he was young, easily swayed into making poor decisions. He'd actually enjoyed doing whatever he wanted to do. Why should he worry about right or wrong?

Now he would sit behind these steel doors for several years. Each day he'd be reminded of his careless lifestyle and the many decisions that had put him there.

God has given us the Bible to help us know how to live a life that pleases Him—a life that also gives us joy and peace. Jesus, of course, is the best example of a human life lived in accord with the heavenly Father. If we live according to God's Word and follow Jesus' example, we can know we are walking the path of righteousness and joy that our Father wants us to follow.

Father, as I read Your Word, show me how to live for You each day. I praise You for coming to show me the way through Your Son, Jesus. Fully God and fully Man, He lived the perfect life on our behalf and offered the perfect sacrifice for our sin. Continue to conform me to His image, O Lord! In His name, amen.

Passing the Faith Along

Teaching them to observe all things that I have commanded you; and lo, I am with you always, even to the end of the age. Amen (Matthew 28:20, *New King James Version*).

Scripture: Matthew 28:16-20
Song: "Tell Me the Story of Jesus"

The father's retirement was fast approaching. After 60 years of running the family business that his great-grandfather had started, his son would soon replace him. For months he had been teaching his son all the business practices that had proven successful through the generations. He covered every detail, making sure his son understood every aspect of the business.

He recalled his own father's guidance and instruction all those years ago. Now his son needed to hear that same wisdom. If the young man ignored or strayed from these guidelines, the company would surely see hard times.

God's Word contains all we need to build and maintain a successful life. Jesus' teachings give us the blueprint. And we too must make sure future generations are taught how to follow Jesus. We can start by telling our children and grandchildren how God has been faithful to us and our family's generations before us.

Let's tell others about the joy in serving and worshipping God. How good it is to live in His ways, enjoying His favor!

O God, Creator of Heaven and earth, thank You for giving us Your Word to show how to live a life pleasing to You. May I faithfully pass along to others the teachings Jesus gave. May future generations know of Your faithfulness to Your people. In the holy name of Jesus, my Lord and Savior, I pray. Amen.

No More Time for Debate

I the LORD will be their God, and my servant David will be prince among them. I the LORD have spoken (Ezekiel 34:24).

Scripture: Ezekiel 34:23-31
Song: "Forever Settled in the Heavens"

For days the lawyers had dramatically presented their cases before the judge. Witnesses had been thoroughly questioned, the defendant had steadfastly declared his innocence, and the district attorney passionately presented every piece of evidence to support the charges. The courtroom atmosphere would be full of tears and accusations one minute and then swiftly change to denials and anger. Each participant gave his or her perception of what happened at the crime scene.

Finally, everyone had been heard, all the evidence presented, and the closing arguments presented. Then the room became completely silent as every face turned to watch the jury foreman. The words he was about to speak were the only ones that mattered. Once the jury spoke, debate would end.

Throughout the Bible, the words "I the LORD have spoken" have indicated God's ultimate authority. Sometimes it was a curse, and sometimes a blessing. Either way, God always has the final word, and there can be no debate. We can trust that what He has said in His Word and what He has promised is true and unshakable. Let's stand on His promises today.

Blessed God, I take comfort in knowing that Your ways and promises are unchangeable. You are faithful to fulfill what You have said, and You alone are holy and just. I worship You as the living, Mighty God! I pray this prayer in the precious name of Jesus my Savior. Amen.

Liberating Faith

When Jesus heard this, he was astonished and said to those following him, "I tell you the truth, I have not found anyone in Israel with such great faith" (Matthew 8:10).

Scripture: Matthew 8:5-13
Song: "He Leadeth Me"

My grandson Benjamin was not ready to take his first swimming lesson. He was dreading his first real encounter with water.

For the first few sessions, he clung to the side of the pool, never moving more than an arm's length away from the edge. But Benjamin had a wise, soft-spoken, gentle teacher.

Within a few weeks, he trusted her implicitly. When she called for him to move away from the pool's edge, he pushed off and swam to her. Benjamin was delighted with himself and with what he had just done.

Today my grandson is a better-than-average swimmer. He enjoys the water. Still, he would not be so ready to jump into the water if his teacher had not instilled in him both faith and trust.

So long as the potential swimmer clutches the side of the pool, he is not swimming. Swimming requires that we lean into the water, trusting that it will hold us up.

People who learn to swim are freed to leave the kiddy pool. They can dive into the deep end. They are liberated to live fully and freely.

Faithful God, give me the grace to face life with courage. Help me to move out because I have placed my trust in You that I may live fully and freely.

August 27–31 **Drexel C. Rankin** served as an ordained minister for more than 35 years with full-time pastorates in Indiana, Alabama, and Kentucky.

The Word Is Near

But what does it say? "The word is near you; it is in your mouth and in your heart" (Romans 10:8a).

Scripture: Romans 10:8-17
Song: "Surely the Presence"

I stood in line at a fast-food restaurant. In front of me were a preschooler and a middle-aged man with a cast on his right arm.

"What's that?" the lad asked.

"It's a cast," the man responded.

"Did it hurt?"

"Well, it did, but it doesn't hurt any more."

"Will you ever get the cast off?"

"Oh, yes. It's going to be as good as new real soon."

For a few moments, it seemed like the conversation was over, until the youngster came back with a very concerned look on his face. "Mister," he asked, "how will you brush your teeth?"

After a moment of hearty laughter by folks nearby, the man said, "Oh, it's a little difficult, but I use my left hand."

I need to ask the same kind of question which that little boy posed. When I see the hurt, the pain, the debilitation in the world, I need to stop and ask the question: "How will you brush your teeth?" I also need to ask that question when I see the opportunity to discover something amazingly new in my own life.

Maybe brushing my teeth with my left hand is how God is trying to push me into new insight. But unless I recognize God's nearness, I'll never understand that.

God, help me to experience Your presence wherever I am. May Your nearness fill me with joy and understanding.

Giving Light

"I no longer live, but Christ lives in me. The life I live in the body, I live by faith in the Son of God, who loved me and gave himself for me" (Galatians 2:20).

Scripture: Galatians 2:15-21
Song: "Shine, Jesus, Shine"

I was cleaning out a desk drawer yesterday afternoon when I found a flashlight that I hadn't used in at least a year or more. I flipped the switch but wasn't surprised when it gave no light. I unscrewed the lens and shook the flashlight to get the batteries out. They wouldn't budge. All four batteries were wedged tightly inside.

Finally, after some effort and some scraping and prying, they came loose. What a mess! Battery acid had corroded the entire inside of the flashlight. The batteries were new when I had put them in—and I had stored the flashlight in a safe, warm place.

There was just one major problem. Batteries and flashlights aren't made to be warm and comfortable. They are designed to be turned on. They are made to give off light.

I am the flashlight filled with fresh batteries. I wasn't created to be warm, safe, and comfortable. I was made by my Creator to be "turned on"—to put His love to work, to apply patience in difficult and trying situations, to ease the pain where there is hurt—and to let my light shine where it is most needed.

God of light, may Your light shine from my life that I might bless others and bring honor and glory to Your name.

The Tests of Life

Examine yourselves to see whether you are in the faith: test yourselves. Do you not realize that Christ Jesus is in you—unless, of course, you fail the test? (2 Corinthians 13:5).

Scripture: 2 Corinthians 13:5-10
Song: "My Faith Looks Up to Thee"

Testing is a normal part of life. It is something that we usually take for granted. I am subjected to all sorts of tests during my lifetime: academic, medical, professional.

If I want to drive my automobile, I must take a written test, a driving test, and an eye exam to get my driver's license. When I had completed my doctoral work in seminary, I needed to pass my oral exam. When I saw my doctor this week, he ordered a blood draw to test my cholesterol level.

There are personal tests that I have faced in life: financial obligations, cancer, broken dreams, peer pressure, seeming failures. I am confronted every day with tests. Some of them I summon. Some assault me.

My response reveals an attitude toward predicaments that invade my life. But isn't that what each day of my life amounts to—a test of faith?

Do I reflect the light of Christ into the darkness of other people's lives? Will the world be a better place for my having lived in it?

Life is not always easy. Often it is overwhelming. But Christ calls me to rise to the challenge rather than to shrink from it in despair and hopelessness.

Lord God, fill me with faith and never let me be without hope. Give me boldness and confidence to be a faithful follower who makes my world a better place.

The Gift of Hope

And we rejoice in the hope of the glory of God . . . and hope does not disappoint us (Romans 5:2b, 5a).

Scripture: Romans 5:1-5
Song: "It Is Well with My Soul"

There is little problem when there are earthly reasons to hope: when the marriage is good, when the job seems secure, when the grades are superior, when we are winning victories.

But where does hope come from when you're disheartened, when endings loom, when roads make abrupt turns into the haze of the unknown?

As we attempt to battle our way through the daily routines, we make a great effort to try to get life together so that we'll have a trouble-free existence. We long for a time when we have solved all our problems and we are free of concerns.

But it never happens quite that way, does it? We become discouraged. We are tempted with self-berating because we are not better—or circumstances are not better.

Hope comes from facing life and its changes honestly and directly. Hope makes us bold and daring. It broadens our horizons to include challenges we'd never attempt on our own. We no longer plan according to what we can see or what our minds can encompass. Rather, we plan with hope and faith.

The gift of hope enables us to live expectantly, knowing that Christ is in charge. I face challenges by keeping hope alive. It's a choice.

Anchor my soul in hope, **Dear Lord**. Help me to weather the challenges that will face me when I least expect them. Freed from anxieties, may I know the joy of serving You in meaningful demonstrations of caring and sharing. In the spirit of Christ, I ask this. Amen.